# ON VIOLENCE

# ON VIOLENCE

## A PHILOSOPHICAL DIALOGUE

Nicholas J. Pappas

Algora Publishing
New York

Library of Congress Cataloging-in-Publication Data

Names: Pappas, Nicholas J., author.
Title: On violence : a philosophical dialogue / Nicholas J. Pappas.
Description: New York : Algora Publishing, [2022] | Summary: "Violence and
    reason are related, if only because violence is done to reason every
    single day. All it takes is to fail to listen. Everything else, all the
    real violence, starts right there, including tough talk in lieu of
    rational argument and the violence of not allowing us to think things
    through. In a virtual conversation with other thoughtful people, we can
    evaluate and refine our own positions, gaining clarity and confidence"--
    Provided by publisher.
Identifiers: LCCN 2022016537 (print) | LCCN 2022016538 (ebook) | ISBN
    9781628944853 (trade paperback) | ISBN 9781628944860 (hardcover) | ISBN
    9781628944877 (pdf)
Subjects: LCSH: Violence--Philosophy. | Reason.
Classification: LCC B844 .P37 2022  (print) | LCC B844  (ebook) | DDC
    179.7--dc23/eng/20220518
LC record available at https://lccn.loc.gov/2022016537
LC ebook record available at https://lccn.loc.gov/2022016538

Printed in the United States

## More Books by Nick Pappas
## from Algora Publishing

Controvert, or On the Lie  and Other Philosophical Dialogues, 2008

Aristocrat, and The Community: Two Philosophical Dialogues, 2010

On Awareness: A Collection of Philosophical Dialogues, 2011

Belief and Integrity: Philosophical Dialogues, 2011

On Strength, 2012

On Freedom: A Philosophical Dialogue, 2014

On Life: Philosophical Dialogues, 2015

On Love: A Philosophical Dialogue, 2016

On Destiny: A Philosophical Dialogue, 2016

On Wisdom: A Philosophical Dialogue, 2017

All of Health: A Philosophical Dialogue, 2018

On Education: A Philosophical Dialogue, 2018

On Power: A Philosophical Dialogue, 2019

On Ideas: A Philosophical Dialogue, 2020

On Passivity: A Philosophical Dialogue, 2021

On Authority: A Philosophical Dialogue, 2021

# TABLE OF CONTENTS

# INTRODUCTION

This book starts with a call to reason. Violence and reason are related, if only because violence is done to reason every single day. It is simple to do violence to reason. All we have to do is fail to listen. Everything else, all the real violence, starts right there. Does that mean, in beginning with reason, I invite violence to be done? After all, I know that there are many people who will not listen to the reason presented in this book. Yes, you might say—but opinions vary concerning reason. What seems reasonable to me might not seem reasonable to you. What do we do with this dilemma? Do both sides of the debate have recourse to violence in the end? Maybe it does not have to be that way. Maybe we can escape from our side and become some sort of neutral observer or, more likely, an open-minded participant in the scene. But to participate is to engage, and if we engage concerning reason we are more or less back on a side. So do we simply observe? Do we become voyeurs of what, in the end, amounts to political life? If so, do we not become effete? Worse, do we become so completely disengaged that we have no concern with the outcomes of politics?

No one can be that disengaged without one of two things. One, there is some other area of concern, which, if examined closely, would reveal itself as another form of politics. Two, the disengaged are so disengaged that they are utterly corrupt or decadent to the extreme. Do we have such people in our midst? Who would they be? Academics in their ivory tower? But academics today are more political than ever before—so much so, the ivory tower might seem to many to be attractive again. Who else can sink to the depths we have in mind? The ultra-rich? They certainly have the means. But they are tied to their means. Their means consume them, for the most part. They often give themselves to their money, to put it plainly. They cannot break away and be completely neutral to the regime and its affairs—for money is the major affair. So who else? Who are these bogeymen, decadent and corrupt?

Philosophers are suspect here, they and their theories. After all, how can you diagnose the ills of a society clearly while being too firmly rooted to it in your own heart? How can you gain critical distance while so attached? And so, we believe, they detach. Does Director, the philosopher in this book, detach? Not to spoil the ending, but Director acknowledges to his interlocutor that he himself is not wholly open. In fact, he has never come across someone who is so. What does this mean? Are decadents not wholly open? If not, what makes them close? Could it be that the interests we have—and all of us have interests—render it impossible to open up fully? Director tries to do this, when he is alone. But when he does he always realizes he has something to learn, something that prevents his opening up in full. Is it ignorance that allows us to think of ourselves as wholly open to either, or any, side?

The threat of violence tears us away from meditations like this. No one is neutral at the point of a gun, unless that person wishes to die. Socrates had a death wish, they say. When he saw himself at the point of the Athenian gun, was he free, if only for that fleeting time in his life? Protégé asks Director why he only attempts to be fully open when he is alone. Director tells him he is afraid of his own violence, that his violence will show. All of us, he says, have truths we violate. The difference is—some of us know which ones.

I hope you enjoy the book.
Nick Pappas

# On Violence

==========

## ~ REASON

*Protégé:* All violence stems from a rebellion against reason.

*Director:* That suggests reason somehow rules. Yet reason to me is a quiet voice, a sweet and gentle voice. How often does such a voice rule?

*Protégé:* What kind of voice rules?

*Director:* More often than not? A loud one. Sometimes a rough one.

*Protégé:* Can loud and rough voices speak with reason?

*Director:* Can they? Yes. Do they? Rarely.

*Protégé:* But people often take them as reason.

*Director:* True. So there's 'reason' and then there's reason.

*Protégé*: And people drown out reason with 'reason'.

*Director*: Yes. But reason keeps on talking away in its small voice. We just have to listen.

*Protégé*: I think reason's constant chatter drives some people crazy. Drives them to violent acts.

*Director*: Is reason to blame?

*Protégé*: Of course not. Their failure to listen is to blame.

*Director*: Do you think failure to listen—to our own reason or the reason of others—is a sort of violence to reason?

*Protégé*: Definitely. It's the only kind of violence to reason there is.

*Director*: But do you agree that reason is sometimes extraordinarily hard to listen to?

*Protégé*: I do. But that's no excuse for the violence we do.

*Director*: You set the bar high.

*Protégé*: That's only fitting—because listening to reason is the ultimate expression of free will.

*Director*: How so?

*Protégé*: Free will means we have a choice, right?

*Director*: Right.

*Protégé*: Well, with reason we always have a choice—to listen or not.

*Director*: But why is this choice the ultimate expression of free will? I can think of other important choices.

*Protégé*: All the other choices we have in life can be taken away. This one can't.

*Director*: Oh, I don't know. Can't we say we always have the choice to be true to ourselves? That seems pretty important to me, and to be a choice that can't be taken away.

*Protégé*: Yes, but it's reason that tells us to stay true!

*Director*: Is it? I sometimes think it's a feeling. Regardless, maybe we should say listening to reason is not the ultimate, but rather the most fundamental, expression of free will.

*Protégé*: That's fine with me.

*Director*: And we're sure no one can take our choice to listen or not away?

*Protégé*: We're sure. No matter how hard they try.

*Director*: And they try very hard.

*Protégé*: Yes, they certainly do.

### ~ CHOICES

*Director*: They want to snuff out reason and tell us what to think.

*Protégé*: Of course. How often do you think they succeed?

*Director*: Many give up and give in.

*Protégé*: But that's the only way for them to succeed, right? You have to give in.

*Director*: Yes, you have to give in.

*Protégé*: Is there ever a time when listening to reason is easy?

*Director*: There is. Sometimes it's easy; sometimes it's hard. We have to take it as it comes. Though I will say this—practice can help.

*Protégé*: But we need to find a way to go off on our own so we can listen. Noise from outside can make listening very hard.

*Director*: I think that's true, *Protégé*. And as you know, it's not always easy to find ways to go off on our own. And even if we're left alone, there's no guarantee we'll listen.

*Protégé*: We have to choose to listen.

*Director*: Yes. And sometimes that's a painful choice.

*Protégé*: True. What do you think makes for the pain?

*Director*: Our emotions have false attachments.

*Protégé*: What does that mean?

*Director*: We think something is good that's bad. And we build up feelings around this view.

*Protégé*: And when reason quietly says the bad thing is bad?

*Director*: We do inner violence to ourselves.

*Protégé*: We don't listen.

*Director*: We try to shut reason up.

*Protégé*: What's the effect of that?

*Director*: Distortions grow in our soul.

*Protégé*: We become deformed?

*Director*: Yes.

*Protégé*: And if this goes on for too long?

*Director*: We can't regain our proper shape.

*Protégé*: We become monstrosities.

*Director*: We lose our hearing, too.

*Protégé*: You mean we can't actually hear reason even if we try?

*Director*: Maybe we can hear, if we truly get quiet enough. But even then, reason might seem to be speaking a foreign tongue.

*Protégé*: So we have to relearn this language which was once our native tongue.

*Director*: Sad but true.

*Protégé*: And if we live in a noisy environment?

*Director*: Then it's that much harder to learn.

*Protégé*: We have to choose quiet over noise, if we hope to hear reason once again.

*Director*: That's the only way.

*Protégé*: But those who have a command of the language of reason, they can choose to enter the noise?

*Director*: If they are master linguists? Yes, they can.

*Protégé*: But why would they?

*Director*: They might be trying to rescue others.

*Protégé*: They pull them aside to where it's quiet and say, 'Listen to this'?

*Director*: Yes, they speak reason aloud.

*Protégé*: Would they ever choose to speak reason in a loud voice? Or is it always more of a whisper?

*Director*: Those who can hear a whisper are more likely to be saved.


~ ALOUD


*Protégé*: I think there's another reason to speak quietly.

*Director*: What reason?

*Protégé*: The noisy ones will do violence to those they hear.

*Director*: What kind of violence?

*Protégé*: Any kind you can imagine. The point is that they make life difficult for them.

*Director*: Hmm. This reminds me of an old criticism of philosophers.

*Protégé*: What criticism?

*Director*: They go off in a corner by themselves and whisper.

*Protégé*: And this is a sign of weakness, sedition, or both?

*Director*: Right.

*Protégé*: And the noisy deaf want to do them harm for this. Well, it's hard to understand. The philosophers do them no harm.

*Director*: True. But the philosophers make themselves targets this way. They have to stay away from corners. And they have to engage.

*Protégé*: They have to speak reason in a steady clear voice.

*Director*: Yes. And then come what may.

*Protégé*: You know, it occurs to me what harm the noisy ones see in the quiet corner.

*Director*: What harm is that?

*Protégé*: They see their young ones are attracted that way.

*Director*: They want their young to be like them, not the philosophers.

*Protégé*: Of course.

*Director*: But when we speak reason in a steady clear voice, we'll be talking to them, the young.

*Protégé*: Then their elders will wish to do us harm, or at least shut us up.

*Director*: Why? Can you say?

*Protégé*: If the young ones grow quiet and listen to the voice of reason inside, it's a condemnation of the elders' way of life.

*Director*: And the elders would do us violence rather than have that happen.

*Protégé*: No doubt they would—whatever sort of violence.

*Director*: Like you said, they want to shut us up. But do you know what's funny?

*Protégé*: Tell me.

*Director*: When I think of an elder, I think of someone frail.

*Protégé*: No, that's a mistake. Elders can be bull-like in their force. 'Elder' is a state of mind.

*Director*: Then maybe I should think of it like this—elders are deaf to reason.

*Protégé*: That's the best definition, yes.

*Director*: And youths?

*Protégé*: Youths can hear quite well.

*Director*: So you can be ninety years old and still be a youth.

*Protégé*: And you can be a bully of ten and be an elder.

*Director*: I'm glad we cleared this up. But I think we're going to have an uphill battle.

*Protégé*: Why?

*Director*: Elders are often associated with wisdom.

*Protégé*: Well, there's 'wisdom' and then there's wisdom.

*Director*: What's the latter?

*Protégé*: Listening to the soft and quiet voice of reason.

*Director*: And the former?

*Protégé*: Getting lucky in your views.

*Director*: What do you mean?

*Protégé*: You tell everyone something will follow from certain things, and it does.

*Director*: What sort of things?

*Protégé*: 'Wisdom' says, for instance, 'Respect your elders or you'll have trouble in life.'

*Director*: Isn't it true?

*Protégé*: But that's not the point.

*Director*: Truth isn't the point?

*Protégé*: There's 'trouble' and then there's trouble, *Director*.

*Director*: I don't doubt there is. But what about us? Are we, the gentle, wise when we speak up?

*Protégé*: How would we be?

*Director*: We counsel people to listen to reason and predict that if they do, things will go well. Or will you tell me there's 'well' and then there's well?

*Protégé*: Many choose 'well' over well, you know.

*Director*: I won't deny I've seen it happen.

*Protégé*: Do you know why they choose 'well'?

*Director*: I don't.

*Protégé*: It's because the deaf bulls gore and stomp to death reason-listening youths.

*Director*: This raises a point I've often wondered about. Must there always be a degree of prudence in all reason?

*Protégé*: You're speaking of another type of wisdom. But let's be clear. The prudence isn't in the reason itself. The prudence is in the delivery of the reason.

*Director*: We have to censor ourselves.

*Protégé*: Yes, of course.

*Director*: Especially when with a youth of not too many years?

*Protégé*: That's a difficult call to make.


~ JUDGMENT


*Director*: How so?

*Protégé*: Well, we want the truth to be known. But the young one might be too young.

*Director*: Suppose he or she isn't.

*Protégé*: Then the problem is that if we speak reason whole, the youth might go back to their elderly bulls and repeat what we said.

*Director*: You mean the youth will tell the truth about the elderly bulls to the elderly bulls.

*Protégé*: Yes. And that can't be good.

*Director*: But if a youth is smart enough to listen to quiet reason, don't you think they'll be smart enough to realize when reason won't be heard?

*Protégé*: Oh, it will be heard—but not understood. Violence will follow.

*Director*: So we tell the youth less than full reason?

*Protégé*: I think we have to, until they prove they can handle reason whole.

*Director*: And by handling reason whole we mean listening to the reason in themselves and venturing further into the core.

*Protégé*: The core of reason? Yes.

*Director*: So if they don't show signs of this, we don't fully share. But if they do, we're free. But this assumes one thing.

*Protégé*: What?

*Director*: That we can tell when they're listening to reason.

*Protégé*: Why couldn't we?

*Director*: Reason might say one thing to them, another to us.

*Protégé*: No. Reason always says the same thing.

*Director*: Does it? I don't see how it can. A reasonable course for me might be madness for you.

*Protégé*: Then how do we determine if someone is listening to reason?

*Director*: They can explain themselves.

*Protégé*: I don't like that.

*Director*: Why not?

*Protégé*: No one should have to defend their reasonings to another.

*Director*: Explaining is different than defending. We can explain to friends why we do what we do. The friends aren't attacking. They simply want to understand.

*Protégé*: Well, that makes sense.

*Director*: And by asking a youth to explain themselves, we inoculate them against the elderly bulls.

*Protégé*: How does that follow?

*Director*: The elders will no doubt ask the youth to explain what he or she means when the youth starts talking reason. The youth will try to explain. But the youth will realize there isn't the same level of understanding there as there was when he or she explained to us here. The youth comes to see that reason, with them, can't be shared. It's something of a natural protection.

*Protégé*: And if the youth suffers a lapse of judgment?

*Director*: What, the youth tells the bulls we spoke reason to her or him? I suppose that happens from time to time. But what really happens in this lapse of judgment?

*Protégé*: The youth tries to speak reason to them.

*Director*: No, I think something else happens. I think the youth tries to forge some sort of compromise. One foot in reason; one foot in violence. If we're confronted with this compromise, we'll deny we had anything to do with it—which is true.

*Protégé*: So what happens to the youth?

*Director*: I think there will be a period of illness. And then it's anyone's guess if he or she will recover.

*Protégé*: Why illness?

*Director*: The inward and outward contradict. Inwardly, the youth recognizes reason. Outwardly, the youth tries to dress reason up to suit the elders. This contradiction is sickening, literally.

*Protégé*: Mental illness.

*Director*: Yes.

*Protégé*: And the youth only gets well when he or she stops trying to have it both ways.

*Director*: That's right. But this is very difficult

*Protégé*: I know it is. The youth has to break away before he or she can get well. But where can the youth go? To a quiet corner somewhere?

*Director*: Something like that, probably. But they'll need to talk to us from time to time.

*Protégé*: I completely agree. But it's just so sad.

*Director*: What is?

*Protégé*: The world is dominated by elders, those who don't listen to reason. Is there any hope this might change?

*Director*: And come to be dominated by reason? I don't know, *Protégé*. But sometimes strange things happen.

## ~ DOMINATION

*Protégé*: What are the obstacles to reason's dominance?

*Director*: I can think of two. One, reason is always gentle. Two, reason always only persuades. Gentle persuasion doesn't want dominance.

*Protégé*: So reason can't dominate because it doesn't want to?

*Director*: Yes, but now you've got me thinking. Maybe reason can dominate in an individual—because the individual wants it to.

*Protégé*: Yes, and let's say it dominates in two individuals, separately. If it can do that, why not three, and then four, and so on?

*Director*: Okay, you have a point. Maybe it really is possible for reason to come to dominate. But I have my doubts.

*Protégé*: What doubts?

*Director*: Well, what usually gets in the way of reason in the individual?

*Protégé*: Passion.

*Director*: Would you have us live without passion?

*Protégé*: Feelings should be moderate, not excessive.

*Director*: Moderate like a gentle summer breeze?

*Protégé*: Yes, exactly.

*Director*: And what about bad feelings?

*Protégé*: They should be like an overcast sky, not some tornado or terrible winter storm.

*Director*: But can we control that? I mean, we feel what we feel and who can say why? What if a cloudy day leaves us feeling depressed, really depressed? And what if a clear blue sky makes us feel so happy that we're manic?

*Protégé*: A person like that is ill and needs help. These feelings will do violence to their reason.

*Director*: And that's the thing with all strong feelings? They do violence to reason?

*Protégé*: Of course.

*Director*: Even strong feelings like love?

*Protégé*: Especially love.

*Director*: You would have our love be mild?

*Protégé*: I would.

*Director*: Really, no passionate love?

*Protégé*: Friendly love is best. It's more constant and reliable. And it doesn't drown out reason. In fact, friendly love stimulates reason.

*Director*: How?

*Protégé*: A friend, a friend who loves us, wants to see us be the best we can be. And so they encourage us to listen to the voice of reason inside.

~ INDIVIDUALS; LOGIC

*Director*: How do they encourage us?

*Protégé*: Through doing what we're doing today.

*Director*: Through dialogue?

*Protégé*: Of course! Don't you agree?

*Director*: I do.

*Protégé*: Dialogue shows The Way.

*Director*: Capital T, capital W?

*Protégé*: Yes. The One True Way.

*Director*: In my experience, dialogue shows individual ways.

*Protégé*: What does that mean?

*Director*: Each individual has unique circumstances, a unique set of facts.

*Protégé*: So dialogue arrives at different truths for each?

*Director*: Yes.

*Protégé*: But if we each had identical facts, impossible as that might be, wouldn't we arrive at the same truths?

*Director*: I don't know.

*Protégé*: But that would mean reason itself varies from person to person! It would mean it's inconsistent!

*Director*: We might not arrive at the same truths while discussing the same facts because of something common to us all.

*Protégé*: What?

*Director*: We all do a certain amount of violence to reason as we listen. And that violence varies—varies in object and amount.

*Protégé*: Is there a way to measure how much violence was done where?

*Director*: We can analyze our thoughts and see where they're illogical. But somebody who's already done violence will be likely to resist.

*Protégé*: This violence can be subtle, can't it?

*Director*: Oh yes, very.

*Protégé*: And it can be tucked away somewhere we can't see.

*Director*: No doubt.

*Protégé*: People often compartmentalize their minds—so they can hide their violence.

*Director*: Are you saying they use logic here; they use logic there; but they refuse to use logic everywhere?

*Protégé*: Of course. Sometimes the most 'logical' are heavily compartmentalized with fortified walls of unreason.

*Director*: And so they do violence to reason in places they think we can't see.

*Protégé*: Yes.

*Director*: But if logic were allowed to flow through the entire mind?

*Protégé*: We would have beauty.

*Director*: I agree. But, you know, most people don't see logic that way.

*Protégé*: No, they see it as intimidating, inhuman even.

*Director*: Yes, and some even see it as doing violence to feeling. But you and I know this isn't so. Logic is sweet, gentle, comforting—when used the proper way.

*Protégé*: Do you think everyone can know the proper way?

*Director*: That's a very hard question. Let me answer you this way—my opinion is that not everyone can. But I'll also say this. You and I both, Protégé, don't always use logic in the proper way.

*Protégé*: I have no doubt about that. But why do you think I don't?

*Director*: Logic to you is sweet and gentle. I can tell this because of the way you employ it in conversation. But I don't think you allow logic to be comforting.

*Protégé*: Sometimes I do. But other times? What if logic whispers to me that I've been going about things all wrong? Is that comforting?

*Director*: Isn't it comforting to learn the truth?

*Protégé*: You don't think truth is sometimes uncomfortable?

*Director*: We have to get used to it, act on it—and then we find comfort.

*Protégé*: Is that something you believe, or something you know through experience?

*Director*: It's something I know through experience. And you?

*Protégé*: It's mostly something I believe. This belief gives me courage to listen to reason. I believe, no matter what I find, that truth is better for me than anything else.


~ Truth


*Director*: More violence is done to truth than anything else.

*Protégé*: Why do you think that is?

*Director*: Ultimately? People don't want others to know they're not listening.

*Protégé*: Listening to reason?

*Director*: Yes. It's like you said. All violence stems from a rebellion against reason.

*Protégé*: But if they're rebelling against reason, why do they care if people know they're not listening to reason?

*Director*: Because for some strange reason, people feel the need to have reason's sanction. They use it to obscure the quotation marks on their 'truth'.

*Protégé*: Why don't they like the truth?

*Director*: Their passions won't have it. And so they commit acts of violence.

*Protégé*: Can you give an example?

*Director*: Ambition, which I believe is a passion.

*Protégé*: Then is it something like this? You think you should be president someday. But reason says otherwise. So instead of listening, you smother the reason in your breast.

*Director*: Yes. And we can substitute any number of things for 'president'.

*Protégé*: People say you just have to believe and you can achieve anything.

*Director*: That's the biggest smothering there is.

*Protégé*: Why? There's power in belief.

*Director*: It takes more than belief.

*Protégé*: It takes the right belief.

*Director*: How so?

*Protégé*: Someone has to be president. So someone must believe. When the right someone believes, that's the right belief.

*Director*: Someone has to be president, sure. But that person has to know, know they can be president, know they should be president—not merely believe.

*Protégé*: How can they know?

*Director*: They have to listen to the quiet voice of reason—all the time. They must commit no acts of violence here.

*Protégé*: But what are we saying? Is belief an act of violence?

*Director*: If it smothers the quiet voice? Yes, of course.

*Protégé*: When is belief appropriate?

*Director*: When we've gone along with reason as far as we can go. When we've hit our honest limit. We stand at a crossroads. We then must choose one way or the other. And then we believe.

*Protégé*: Believe we've made the right choice.

*Director*: Yes.

~ ATTACK

*Protégé*: What if reason later speaks up and says we made the wrong choice?

*Director*: And we've traveled far down our path of choice and belief? I suppose there would be a great temptation to do violence at this point.

*Protégé*: We would do violence to ourselves, inwardly; and then to others who might speak the truth about our way, outwardly.

*Director*: Inward violence to truth almost always precedes outward violence to truth, yes.

*Protégé*: I wish we could make some sort of pre-emptive strike against those who would do violence to truth.

*Director*: How would we know who to strike?

*Protégé*: There must be certain tendencies in speech or deed that would clue us in.

*Director*: What would the strike accomplish?

*Protégé*: It would take away their 'reasonable' sanction for violent acts. After all, we're striking them with reason.

*Director*: Gentle, sweet reason?

*Protégé*: Yes .

*Director*: We don't speak it with force?

*Protégé*: No, Director, we don't.

*Director*: But will they listen?

*Protégé*: Almost certainly not.

*Director*: Then what after this?

*Protégé*: We speak sweet reason with force.

*Director*: So you're saying we give them a chance before we resort to force.

*Protégé*: Yes.

*Director*: Is the force meant to intimidate them?

*Protégé*: Exactly so.

*Director*: If it does?

*Protégé*: They'll be afraid to bring their lies to the world.

*Director*: And maybe then they'll be forced to listen to the reasons inside?

*Protégé*: Right.

*Director*: But if they don't?

*Protégé*: They might attack.

*Director*: And if they do?

*Protégé*: We're justified in using proper force.

*Director*: Physical force?

*Protégé*: If they attack us with physical force, yes. We defend.

*Director*: So the reasonable only use force in defense. But didn't we just speak of pre-emptive attacks?

*Protégé*: Those are mental attacks, *Director*.

*Director*: And mental attacks, forceful mental attacks, do no harm?

*Protégé*: Not when those of reason make them.


## - LET BE

*Director*: Why not just let the violent be?

*Protégé*: Because unreason spreads.

*Director*: What do you mean?

*Protégé*: If you were raised in a house dominated by unreason, wouldn't you learn to be unreasonable?

*Director*: You have a point—though I might rebel.

*Protégé*: Yes, but successful rebels are few. But if I came in with a pre-emptive attack and showed you an alternative point of view?

*Director*: I might learn how best to rebel.

*Protégé*: Yes.

*Director*: But those of my house would almost certainly blame you for my rebellion.

*Protégé*: If they found out it was me. But that's the chance I take.

*Director*: And you're doing this all for me?

*Protégé*: I'm doing this for all of us, me included.

*Director*: And if I learn not to do violence to myself or others, I one day might perform pre-emptive strikes of my own?

*Protégé*: You'd pay it forward, as they say.

*Director*: But rebellion, it's violent in its own way. No?

*Protégé*: Yes, but it's violence in self-defense. And you wouldn't be doing violence to truth. You'd be doing violence to violence.

*Director*: Let's hope a habit of violence doesn't form.

*Protégé*: What do you mean?

*Director*: When a habit of violence forms with those otherwise given to reason, they come to think they have reason when they don't. And if they are having trouble seeing the reason in themselves, how likely are they to see the reason in others?

*Protégé*: Not very. So you're saying they might attack reason, thinking it's unreason?

*Director*: Doesn't it seem likely? A habit of violence renders you blind.

*Protégé*: Can we attack these blind and force them to see?

*Director*: It depends how deeply ingrained the habit of violence is.

*Protégé*: If it's very deeply ingrained?

*Director*: There isn't much we can do.

*Protégé*: And if it's otherwise?

*Director*: We reason with them.

*Protégé*: How do we know what sort of reason to use?

*Director*: We feel our way in—through dialogue.

*Protégé*: And if we meet with a reasoned response?

*Director*: I'd say we've had some success. And we may, if we're lucky, have won a friend. But sometimes it's best to let sleeping dogs lie.

*Protégé*: What do you mean?

*Director*: As we dialogue with another, if we meet too much resistance, with no good signs, we should leave them well enough alone.

*Protégé*: What's a good sign?

*Director*: Deep honesty, fierce integrity, love of justice—these sorts of things.

*Protégé*: People with those sorts of things might resist?

*Director*: Oh, yes. It happens all the time. We have to exercise some patience with them.

*Protégé*: But why wouldn't they listen to reason?

*Director*: Usually? It's because of pride.

*Protégé*: They don't want to admit they're mistaken on certain things.

*Director*: Yes.

*Protégé*: Well, then we'll be patient. But back to the sleeping dogs. They tend to wake up at inopportune times.

*Director*: Yes, I've noticed. What can we do?

*Protégé*: Think of the movies.

*Director*: Okay. I'm thinking of the movies.

*Protégé*: What happens when people want to break into a compound where there are attack dogs on guard?

*Director*: The intruders bring steaks to feed the creatures so they'll leave them alone.

*Protégé*: Yes!

*Director*: So what are you saying? We need to bring intellectual steaks?

*Protégé*: Precisely.

*Director*: But what's an intellectual steak?

*Protégé*: Something juicy they'll love.

*Director*: Like what?

*Protégé*: Something that says doing violence to reason is good.

*Director*: You want us to say that?

*Protégé*: Why not?

*Director*: It has something to do with truth.

*Protégé*: Yes, but we'll slowly lead them to see that the opposite is true.

*Director*: Start one way and finish another?

*Protégé*: We meet them where they're at. Then we walk them to our position.

*Director*: And a dog will take this walk once fed?

*Protégé*: If it won't, no harm. We'll just let it be.


### ~ Violence


*Director*: What argument is there that says doing violence to reason is good?

*Protégé*: It starts with this. Reason is nothing other than the thoughts or reasons of others. To be reasonable means to surrender and allow these reasons to have their sway.

*Director*: And what are reasons?

*Protégé*: Particular demands of the body and soul. We project these onto others as reasons. Those who don't go along are unreasonable.

*Director*: So it's good to fight reason, to resist those selfish demands.

*Protégé*: Yes, of course.

*Director*: Fight it in others, okay. But do we also fight it in ourselves?

*Protégé*: We do—because we have pride. Force in getting what you want is more honest than reason's deceits.

*Director*: How exactly does reason deceive?

*Protégé*: It takes something that is particular and generalizes it, universalizes it.

*Director*: The particular being what a particular individual wants.

*Protégé*: Right.

*Director*: Okay. But let's get back to force. That can be either language-based or physical?

*Protégé*: Language is physical. It comes from our mouths, kisses the air, and strikes the ear.

*Director*: So violence is violence no matter the means.

*Protégé*: Yes. And it's all in self-defense against the impositions of reason.

*Director*: That's their position. How do we walk them to ours?

*Protégé*: We try sweet and gentle reason with them.

*Director*: What do we say? 'We don't want anything from you other than for you to listen to reason'?

*Protégé*: More or less? Yes.

*Director*: And if that doesn't work?

*Protégé*: Then we know our enemy.

*Director*: What should we do with this enemy? I mean, they weren't impressed by our impressive reasoning.

*Protégé*: Oh, you know we'd offer much more reason than what you just said.

*Director*: But that's our basic point.

*Protégé*: True.

*Director*: So what can we do?

*Protégé*: Undermine them in other ways.

*Director*: Why not open attack?

*Protégé*: How would an open attack look? 'You're not reasonable! Take that!'

*Director*: I was thinking we might do better than that.

*Protégé*: But we're talking about someone with no inner allegiance to reason. Our words have no point of purchase with them. We're forced to resort to other means.

*Director*: Like what?

*Protégé*: We search out those around this person. We see if reason holds sway with any of them.

*Director*: And if so?

*Protégé*: We find ways to have them work with us to rein the violent one in.

*Director*: That sounds good to me. But this can't become a passion with us. Unreason lies that way.

*Protégé*: No, it's simple policy, not passion.

*Director*: Good. But, Protégé, remind me why we're doing all this.

*Protégé*: Unreason spreads. We have to nip it in the bud—for the sake of those committed to reason, anywhere in the world.

*Director*: Yes, the ripples of unreason travel far and wide. But what are we talking about in concrete terms?

*Protégé*: Let me give you an example. Someone who is violent toward reason holds a position of influence and seeks one greater still. We, in our reason, prevent their success.

*Director*: What means do we employ?

*Protégé*: Any sanctioned by reason.

*Director*: What if your reason says to use whatever—and I mean whatever— means at your disposal; but mine says to only use honest means?

*Protégé*: Then reason says—speak nothing to you of means.


~ SHARING


*Director*: I think that's a mistake.

*Protégé*: Why?

*Director*: Because if you speak to me of means, I might talk you out of making a bigger mistake.

*Protégé*: That could be. But how would you stop me?

*Director*: If you're open with me, I can reason with you.

*Protégé*: Why wouldn't I be open?

*Director*: Because you're bent on what you want to do, and you know I don't approve. But I think there's more.

*Protégé*: Oh?

*Director*: It has to do with how close we are to the light.

*Protégé*: How can we determine who is closer—and if closer, I assume, therefore right?

*Director*: Through dialogue.

*Protégé*: Ah, dialogue again. What's the point of dialogue?

*Director*: To help each other see.

*Protégé*: Yes, but saying is one thing; seeing is another. Saying through dialogue can help lead someone to see, but sight must come on its own.

*Director*: We're in violent agreement.

*Protégé*: And what if I see but you don't? Do I have to wait for you to catch up?

*Director*: No, waiting does no good. You must proceed.

*Protégé*: Toward the light.

*Director*: Yes, and then you must share the light.

*Protégé*: Even with laggard you?

*Director*: With everyone with eyes to see.

*Protégé*: Even though they don't yet see.

*Director*: You hope to make an impression.

*Protégé*: With the hope that one day they'll understand.

*Director*: Right.

*Protégé*: And when they do?

*Director*: You get confirmation that what you both see is actually light.

*Protégé*: What else could it be?

*Director*: Haven't you heard of putting things in a false light?

*Protégé*: Of course I have.

*Director*: That's what we're guarding against.

*Protégé*: So what happens if we confirm our light is true?

*Director*: We have a bit more confidence.

*Protégé*: That's it?

*Director*: That's much.

*Protégé*: And now what? We just start all over again? We share this light with another with eyes to see? To gain even more confidence?

*Director*: Yes, and after a few more sharings like this we might be ready to share where light is less likely to be known.

*Protégé*: Because we'll take every chance.

*Director*: That's right.

*Protégé*: We'd have to know the light very well for this.

*Director*: Very well indeed. And we have to be careful.

*Protégé*: Why?

*Director*: There's a temptation to do violence here.

*Protégé*: How so? We'll be attacked?

*Director*: Maybe. But what I was thinking is that we might try to force what we know on others.

*Protégé*: The square peg in the round hole?

*Director*: Something like that. The point is that we must not alter the truth to suit the needs at hand.

*Protégé*: But we all do this every day.

*Director*: 'We all' is not who I'm talking to.

*Protégé*: Point taken.

*Director*: When I'm talking to not-we-all, I am very careful to tell it like it is. No exaggeration. No emotional push or coloring. No cutting corners. No cowardice.

*Protégé*: Yes, but what if while you're doing this you realize they're not ready to understand?

*Director*: I speak the reasoned truth—and hope for what the future will bring.

*Protégé*: It sounds like you have a lot of hope.

*Director*: If I didn't, I would never open my mouth to share.

*Protégé*: This is interesting. You only share when there's hope?

*Director*: Yes. And my sense of hope refines as I learn more about life.

*Protégé*: But, Director, are you sharing more or less as you learn?

*Director*: With some I share more; with some I share... less.

## ~ More or Less

*Protégé*: Where do you share more?

*Director*: Where there is less violence.

*Protégé*: And less? Where there is more?

*Director*: Yes. But to be clear, I share quite a bit even there.

*Protégé*: What do you share?

*Director*: The conclusions.

*Protégé*: And what about the reasons, the reasonings?

*Director*: Those go to those of less violence, my friend.

*Protégé*: What's a conclusion you share with the more violent?

*Director*: That they are wasting their lives.

*Protégé*: And if they reply that they are merely violent in self-defense?

*Director*: I'd say, 'We should destroy ourselves in order to defend ourselves?'

*Protégé*: And if they ask what kind of destruction you're talking about?

*Director*: Destruction of the inner self as articulated by the inner voice.

*Protégé*: But they'll object that the inner voice isn't ourselves.

*Director*: What is it?

*Protégé*: Something that comes from somewhere else. Angels or devils whispering in our ear. You know. That's what they say.

*Director*: Do you believe that?

*Protégé*: I suppose it's possible. But many would say the inner voice is the soul. I'm inclined that way. And if the soul is immortal, so is the voice. Do you believe the soul is immortal?

*Director*: I don't believe it, but I'm open to the possibility.

*Protégé*: Do you believe reason is immortal?

*Director*: Are you asking if I believe in Reason with a capital R?

*Protégé*: Do you?

*Director*: I don't.

*Protégé*: Then let me ask you this. Would you promote Reason with a capital R if you thought it would result in less violence to reason with a lower case R?

*Director*: But that very act would result in violence to reason with a lower case R. Reason, as far as I can tell, shows that there is no Reason with a capital R. Should I do violence to that?

*Protégé*: No, you have a point. But this is interesting. People can speak in the name of Reason and do violence to reason?

*Director*: Yes, of course. It happens all the time. One of the tricks is to speak 'logically' but to only reason on some of the facts. The problematic facts are swept aside—violently.

*Protégé*: And if you bring up these missing facts?

*Director*: Violence is done to you.

*Protégé*: When is the violence more, and when is it less?

*Director*: It's less when little is at stake. In a private meeting, for instance. It's more when more is at stake. In a public gathering, for example.

*Protégé*: In a public gathering, they probably feel that not to do violence to you for bringing up these facts would be to admit they are facts.

*Director*: I think there's truth in that. Silence here might mean agreement, consent. Or so they fear. And so they attack.

*Protégé*: Are fear and violence more or less related?

*Director*: When some people fear they lash out. When others fear they reach within.

*Protégé*: What sort of person are you?

*Director*: When I fear I try with all my might to listen to reason, to do whatever I can to get to a place where I can hear, so I know what to do. How about you?

*Protégé*: I have to admit—sometimes I lash out with reasons against that which makes me fear.

*Director*: Sometimes I speak reasons, but I don't lash out. I speak in as calm and gentle a voice as I can command.

*Protégé*: I have a hard time doing that.

*Director*: All we can do is our best.

*Protégé*: I'll try harder.

*Director*: But, Protégé, I should tell you—sometimes reason tells me to shout, to shout as loud as I can.

*Protégé*: It all depends, doesn't it, *Director*?

*Director*: Yes, it does.

### ~ Like with Like

*Protégé*: We have to meet violence with violence.

*Director*: That's usually true.

*Protégé*: When wouldn't it be true?

*Director*: When we have a platform on which to stand.

*Protégé*: What do you mean?

*Director*: Suppose you're with a group of friends, friends of reason. And suppose a violent man comes up and assaults you with his words. Should you be violent in return?

*Protégé*: You don't have to be because you have the backing of your friends.

*Director*: So I could speak reason to him in the hope the words might strike home.

*Protégé*: I suppose there's a chance.

*Director*: Yes, and if not now, maybe in a month from now as he reflects on the scene.

*Protégé*: Unlikely, but possible.

*Director*: But now let's take away the friends. Can't I do the same thing?

*Protégé*: The situation is more dangerous without the friends.

*Director*: True, but can't I do the same?

*Protégé*: I suppose you could.

*Director*: And might my words have more appeal to the other absent the embarrassment of being reasoned with in front of a gathering?

*Protégé*: Possibly.

*Director*: And what danger is there really? Physical attack?

*Protégé*: Of course physical attack. With your friends there the risk is much less.

*Director*: What's riskier, and likely to escalate the situation? To speak gentle words of reason, or to shout back at the top of my lungs?

*Protégé*: The latter.

*Director*: But if he were to attack me physically no matter my gentle words, I would meet that violence with violence of my own.

*Protégé*: But you can take that chance.

*Director*: What do you mean?

*Protégé*: You know how to defend yourself. I don't.

*Director*: So you would shout?

*Protégé*: No, I would flee—before I even uttered words of reason.

*Director*: With you, reason wouldn't be given a chance.

*Protégé*: It wouldn't. Not with the man of violence, anyway.

*Director*: Do you often flee?

*Protégé*: Literally? No. But figuratively? Honestly? Yes. I'm afraid of violence in all its forms.

*Director*: Are you a... coward?

*Protégé*: I think I might be.

*Director*: It's not cowardice to be afraid.

*Protégé*: But it's cowardice to run away.

*Director*: No, sometimes we have to run away.

*Protégé*: Yes, but not every time.

*Director*: Who knows? Maybe every time so far you had to run away.

*Protégé*: Why?

*Director*: Because you weren't ready.

*Protégé*: What would make me ready?

*Director*: Gaining confidence by having conversations like this.

*Protégé*: With those like me? Those devoted to reason?

*Director*: Yes, of course. Where do you think I found my confidence? Through dialogue, my friend. But you can't just say something once. You have to say it over and over again, hear it over and over again. It's training, and who doesn't need some of that?

## ~ ALONE

*Protégé*: I think I see the problem. I'm something of a loner. It's just my books and me. No dialogue here.

*Director*: Books are good. And if they're the right books, you can dialogue with them. In fact, I strongly suspect you've done that before.

*Protégé*: Yes, but I need friends, friends who think like me.

*Director*: Friends are good, too. And necessary. But do you know what's wonderful about friends?

*Protégé*: Tell me.

*Director*: They create habits.

*Protégé*: I don't understand.

*Director*: When you interact with the right kind of friends, you form patterns of behavior. In our case, cherishing reason and all that implies.

*Protégé*: What does it imply?

*Director*: When our friends encounter reason, they smile and feel that sweet summer breeze. When they encounter violence, they frown and look up and see the overcast sky.

*Protégé*: How will that help me?

*Director*: Over time you'll tend to react like them. When you encounter violence on your own, you won't feel a tornado of fear inside. You may well feel fear, but as the gloom of a cloudy day. You can handle a cloudy day. You can't handle a tornado.

*Protégé*: I think you're exactly right. I do feel a tornado of fear. I would love for it only to be a cloudy sky.

*Director*: Form a habit of reason with friends. It will serve you well—both with them and when you're alone.

*Protégé*: You can tell how someone acts when they're alone, can't you?

*Director*: What do you mean?

*Protégé*: I mean, it's written into their character, isn't it?

*Director*: There's truth in what you say.

*Protégé*: So if I hadn't said I'm a coward, you still would have known.

*Director*: I would have known you could do with some practice.

*Protégé*: But the fact is I still don't know how to defend myself.

*Director*: You can learn that, too. I can teach you.

*Protégé*: You really would?

*Director*: Of course.

*Protégé*: Are you talking about physical self-defense or mental self-defense?

*Director*: When you're accomplished in both, it's hard to tell the difference.

*Protégé*: But a punch in the nose is a punch in the nose.

*Director*: Yes, but there's a mind that told that fist to punch. There's a lot of reason behind a well-directed blow.

*Protégé*: And there are mental punches?

*Director*: Certainly. And throws, and holds, and so on.

*Protégé*: I want to learn them all.

*Director*: I'll show you what I can.

*Protégé*: What can't you show me?

*Director*: Your reasons why you would kick, grab, and fight.

*Protégé*: Why not?

*Director*: Because that you have to come up with on your own.

*Protégé*: But why?

*Director*: Because the facts of your life are different than mine. Reason says different facts require different courses of action.

*Protégé*: So we're all alone in the end.

*Director*: In one sense. But in another, when we have friends, we're never alone. Even when we're alone.

*Protégé*: How can you say that?

*Director*: True friends are always with us—even if they're dead. They hold a place in our memories, our hearts. Surely you know this.

*Protégé*: I'm not sure I've ever had a true friend.

*Director*: Well, let me be one. And this will make the training go better.

*Protégé*: I don't doubt it will. But promise me one thing?

*Director*: What?

*Protégé*: You won't soon be dead.


~ DEATH


*Director*: Death is a funny thing.

*Protégé*: How so?

*Director*: Some people are only born when they die.

*Protégé*: What does that mean?

*Director*: The fruits of their life ripen only then.

*Protégé*: Why wouldn't they ripen while they're alive?

*Director*: I have to drop the metaphor. It's because they hide their wonderful deeds.

*Protégé*: Why would they do that?

*Director*: Modesty.

*Protégé*: Modesty? I don't understand. Why take modesty to such an extreme?

*Director*: It's a form of prudence.

*Protégé*: Prudence against what?

*Director*: Violence to those deeds. And now I'll pick up the metaphor again. The deeds are like planted seeds. When the shoots come up, they're all too easily trampled upon. The doer of such deeds wants the seeds to be strong before they're known.

*Protégé*: That makes sense. But what does this mean for me? Are you saying my deeds are like this?

*Director*: This sort of thing happens from time to time. It may be that some of your deeds will be like this. The point is that you mustn't think this is somehow wrong. To the contrary. It can be good, very good. And sometimes great.

*Protégé*: Do you have seeds you have to believe will grow?

*Director*: What an interesting way to put it. Let me answer you with this. Farmers know that under the right circumstances, most of their seeds will grow. Under bad circumstances, some of the seeds will grow.

*Protégé*: And under terrible circumstances none of them will grow.

*Director*: That's true. But truly terrible circumstances are relatively rare. So odds are good at least some of our seeds will grow. But we have to take the lesson from this.

*Protégé*: What lesson?

*Director*: We can't become overly attached to any one of our seeds. We simply don't know which seeds will sprout and grow.

*Protégé*: So we should plant as many seeds as we can.

*Director*: Well, not quite. We shouldn't become fanatical here.

*Protégé*: Why not?

*Director*: Because there's more to life than planting seeds. We should take the time to eat the fruits of others. After all, isn't that what we hope will happen to our fruits one day?

*Protégé*: That's a very good point.

*Director*: Yes, but this talk was all about death. There are many crops we can harvest while we're alive.

*Protégé*: And many feasts to be had.

*Director*: That's the spirit! And how lovely it would be to feast in the open air while tickled by a gentle summer breeze.

*Protégé*: Tell me something, Director. When we reach winter, do our reasons slowly die or are they with us until the end?

*Director*: It varies. And it's hard to say why.

*Protégé*: I expect you to speak the hard.

*Director*: Here's how it seems to me. If we've had our reasons all our lives, they only die when we do. Yes, details fade. But the main thrusts will be there still, if only as habits of soul.

*Protégé*: But if we change reasons midway through?

*Director*: Then the habits won't be as strong.

*Protégé*: And we might revert to earlier habits?

*Director*: If they were deeply ingrained in the soul? Yes, that seems likely.

*Protégé*: But if we really practice and strive?

*Director*: There's a very good chance our reasons will stay with us 'til the end.


## ~ REASONS


*Director*: But listen to us. Reason is reason. And here we are speaking of reasons.

*Protégé*: What do you mean? What's wrong with reasons?

*Director*: Reasons are usually involved in making a case for or against something. Reason is something more.

*Protégé*: So what should we do?

*Director*: Ignore the reasons and listen to reason. Many don't learn to listen to reason until they reach middle age or later.

*Protégé*: And some people listen right away? Is it possible for someone to have always listened to reason? Have you?

*Director*: All of us have been guilty at one time or another of doing violence to reason. With reason there's no such thing as a saint.

*Protégé*: Yes, but on the whole?

*Director*: On the whole? Some learn to listen at a very young age. But there are difficulties that come with this. Conflicts.

*Protégé*: I can see that.

*Director*: Yes, and conflicts, if not properly handled, can lead to distortions of reason.

*Protégé*: You make a good point.

*Director*: But I'll say, on the whole, it's better to listen sooner rather than later.

*Protégé*: Point taken.

*Director*: And I have to say more about reasons.

*Protégé*: Please.

*Director*: Reasons derive from reason, but they are not reason themselves. They are artifacts used for the trial.

*Protégé*: What trial?

*Director*: The capital trial of violence versus gentle reason.

*Protégé*: Violence prosecutes us?

*Director*: Of course. Violence would make us look guilty.

*Protégé*: Of what?

*Director*: Going against the dominant, violent emotions of the day.

*Protégé*: So we're guilty?

*Director*: Only if we accept that resistance is a crime.

*Protégé*: And we can only resist with reasons, not reason itself?

*Director*: The court of emotion is deaf to reason. But reasons can be used to poke and prod.

*Protégé*: I think we have to be careful here.

*Director*: We certainly do. We can't lapse into violence ourselves.

*Protégé*: When we poke and prod, what do we hope to accomplish?

*Director*: We hope to knock them off balance so they decide to acquit.

*Protégé*: Has that ever worked before?

*Director*: Not that I'm aware.

*Protégé*: Then why would we do it?

*Director*: What other choice do we have? Be silent? We'll be condemned. Speak sweet reason? It won't be heard. Reasons seem like our only chance.

*Protégé*: No. We have to speak reason. Even if they don't hear, someone else might.

*Director*: And in that someone else, reason might be a seed that one day sprouts?

*Protégé*: Yes.

*Director*: You're encouraging me.

*Protégé*: I'm encouraging you?

*Director*: Of course! What are friends for?


~ FRIENDS


*Director*: The best of friends reason together. That's how they interact.

*Protégé*: What if one is better at reasoning than the other? It's a one-sided friendship then.

*Director*: There is no 'better' when it comes to reason. There's more open, honest—yes. But better? You're not engaged in reason if you're that. There must be give and take. Yes, sometimes one will talk more than the other. But so long as both are engaged, the friendship has more than one side.

*Protégé*: I take your point.

*Director*: I'm glad we cleared this up. But it's hard to find good friends.

*Protégé*: I know. Sometimes we make do with those who can't give and take.

*Director*: Yes, and that's an awful mistake.

*Protégé*: But we learn from our mistakes. Better to make the mistake than live in isolation, no?

*Director*: Some people are afraid of mistakes. Are you?

*Protégé*: Honestly? I... am.

*Director*: Then I hope you're not making a mistake by talking with me!

*Protégé*: Hardly! Of that I'm sure.

*Director*: Then build on that certainty and see where you go.

*Protégé*: Will you help me vet my friends?

*Director*: I can. Bring them around and we'll see how open to reason they are. But I think you can see that on your own, *Protégé*.

*Protégé*: Maybe. But it doesn't hurt to bring them to you.

*Director*: No, that's true. And I would enjoy it. Do you have anyone in mind?

*Protégé*: There is a person in one of my classes who seems open this way.

*Director*: Why haven't you made friends already?

*Protégé*: He's more confident than I am. I get nervous.

*Director*: Okay. So how will the three of us get together?

*Protégé*: There's a coffee shop he goes to after class.

*Director*: What do we do? Just walk up and ask to sit down?

*Protégé*: No, we can't do that. I'm at a loss.

*Director*: What's the subject?

*Protégé*: Subject?

*Director*: Of your course.

*Protégé*: Oh, it's Ancient Greek.

*Director*: I studied a little Greek. Is he good at it in class?

*Protégé*: One of the best.

*Director*: Maybe you can tell him that I'm a continuing education student who is struggling with Greek and could use a little help. Do you think he might bite?

*Protégé*: He has a generous nature. I bet he would. But then what do we do?

*Director*: I'll tell him I'm having trouble with verbs. This part is true. I did have trouble with verbs.

*Protégé*: Who doesn't? What then?

*Director*: I'll get a textbook and ask him to walk me through one of the exercises. And I truly could use a refresher, so no lie here.

*Protégé*: What then?

*Director*: I'll thank him and turn the conversation to general topics about Ancient Greece. They cared a lot about friendship then, you know. We could talk about that.

*Protégé*: That sounds good. But what happens when he learns you're not really a student?

*Director*: Hmm. There's only one thing to do. I'll have to register for a class.

*Protégé*: We're in luck! Registration for continuing education is this week!

*Director*: Excellent! What do you think? Or is this too sneaky for you? You could always just ask him to join you for a cup alone.

*Protégé*: I'd rather do it with you.


~ AGAIN


*Director*: When we talk with him about reason, I think I know what we can do.

*Protégé*: What?

*Director*: We can walk through what we talked about today again with him.

*Protégé*: Just the general themes?

*Director*: Yes, of course. And if he has this generous personality you mentioned, he'll likely jump right in. If it goes well, maybe we can plan to meet once a week.

*Protégé*: Over verbs.

*Director*: Yes, over verbs. We'll have all semester to meet over and over again.

*Protégé*: I think this is a very good idea. But how can you get time off from work?

*Director*: The company believes in continuing education.

*Protégé*: It doesn't matter what course you take? It doesn't have to be relevant to business?

*Director*: The company is liberal in these things.

*Protégé*: Great!

*Director*: Should we practice and go over what we've already said?

*Protégé*: Maybe later. Now I'm wondering if he's had any violence done to him.

*Director*: Haven't we all?

*Protégé*: Maybe. But he doesn't seem to be aware of it if he has.

*Director*: We'll have to ask.

*Protégé*: What, just ask him if he's had violence done to him?

*Director*: And whether he let it affect his reason, yes.

*Protégé*: And if he says no?

*Director*: We'll ask him to prove it.

*Protégé*: Ha! What will we ask him to do to prove it?

*Director*: Reason with us.

*Protégé*: And what will we reason about?

*Director*: I don't know. We'll have to play it by ear. There's no sheet of music for us to follow.

*Protégé*: We really need a topic ready at hand.

*Director*: Why?

*Protégé*: I'm not comfortable to just wing it like this.

*Director*: Okay. Do you still have that audio recorder?

*Protégé*: The one I record my lessons with? I have it with me now.

*Director*: Turn it on.

*Protégé*: You want to hear my lessons?

*Director*: No, I want to record our conversation.

*Protégé*: Why?

*Director*: So you can take it home then think about a topic to have ready at hand, one you'll draw from our talk here today.

*Protégé*: If we're recording I'll be too nervous to talk.

*Director*: Then let's just ask him to reason about his friends.

*Protégé*: Isn't that too personal?

*Director*: No! I'll just say, 'So tell us about your friends.' He'll probably laugh and say something clever.

*Protégé*: And we'll say true friendship is based on reason.

*Director*: We certainly will. If he disagrees, we know what to say.

*Protégé*: And if he agrees?

*Director*: Then we're in luck. And that will be all for the day. You and I can meet later to review what was said and make the plan for our next attack.

*Protégé*: But it's not really an attack.

*Director*: It certainly is. Do you think we'll be satisfied with what he says? We're going to attack any violence we find in him.

*Protégé*: By reasoning with it?

*Director*: By reasoning with the reasonable part of his soul—and hoping his reason comes to attack the violence he has within.


~ WITHIN


*Protégé*: You're saying we're certain he has violence within?

*Director*: In my experience, no one has no violence within. It's just that some of us contain it better than others.

*Protégé*: Can't we eradicate it somehow?

*Director*: It seems like it always comes back.

*Protégé*: Why do you think it does?

*Director*: It could be because of violent pressure from without.

*Protégé*: I know what you mean. Sometimes violence from without makes me feel violent within. What's the best way to deal with this?

*Director*: The best way is probably to get away from the violence without.

*Protégé*: But isn't that the coward's way?

*Director*: I don't think so—unless you're confident you can do something about that violence.

*Protégé*: Maybe with practice I'll have the confidence. But sometimes I can't get away.

*Director*: Then you have to find a way to keep the cancer of violence from taking hold inside.

*Protégé*: What's your way?

*Director*: I try not to listen.

*Protégé*: Is that a good way?

*Director*: There's nothing good about being subjected to violence.

*Protégé*: I know. But there has to be a better way.

*Director*: Then argue with them, the violent. And I don't mean a violent argument. I mean stay composed and gentle and tell them what you think.

*Protégé*: That might cause a break.

*Director*: I thought we wanted to get away.

*Protégé*: Some people you just can't escape.

*Director*: I'm not so sure about that. But let's say it's true. We need to put the relationship on a better footing. The only better footing I know is reason. So how can you help the other be more reasonable?

*Protégé*: I guess the only way is to be patient and keep on speaking gentle reason to them, in hopes they'll learn to follow the example.

*Director*: But you'll say nothing that provokes a break?

*Protégé*: I can't.

*Director*: Okay. You know the facts of your life best. So I guess it's patience for you. And who knows? This might prove to be very good practice.

*Protégé*: You think so?

*Director*: Why not? Even if the person never comes around, you'll learn patient reasoning. Can that be bad?

*Protégé*: Of course not.

*Director*: Then there it is. You might even be able to use this directly on the violence within. Patience with yourself is good, especially when attempting something difficult.

*Protégé*: Are you patient with yourself for the things within?

*Director*: It's very hard to be patient. I don't always succeed.

*Protégé*: What exasperates you?

*Director*: When I find myself making the same old mistakes. I wonder if I'll never learn.

*Protégé*: Why don't you learn?

*Director*: If I knew that, I would learn. But maybe you can help.

*Protégé*: Me? How?

*Director*: I find myself always falling in love. And then I do foolish things.

*Protégé*: What kind of things?

*Director*: I forget myself.

*Protégé*: What does that mean? You forget you're old?

*Director*: Hush! When you're old, tell me how easily you forget that fact.

*Protégé*: Ha, ha! That's it! You think you're young.

*Director*: Do you remember what we said about elders and such? Well, I am young in what counts.

*Protégé*: I believe you. But then what's wrong with forgetting yourself?

*Director*: I sometimes forget the facts of my life and think the facts of my beloved are mine.

*Protégé*: Oh. That sounds serious.

*Director*: It is. And try as I might to remember, I forget. It gets me into trouble.

*Protégé*: I can imagine how. You need someone to remind you.

*Director*: Who?

*Protégé*: Me! So next time you fall in love, call me and I'll be your constant reminder to always be yourself.

*Director*: You would really do this for me?

*Protégé*: Of course! With pleasure. After all, you're helping me with friends.

*Director*: We have a deal. We'll help shore each other up, both without and within.

## ~ REINFORCEMENT

*Director*: This reminds me of something. Do you remember what we said about habit?

*Protégé*: We said a few things, yes.

*Director*: Habit shores us up much as the help of a friend.

*Protégé*: Habit reinforces reason.

*Director*: Yes, but there's a great danger here.

*Protégé*: What danger?

*Director*: Reason is supple. Habit is not.

*Protégé*: Habit might interfere with reason.

*Director*: Yes, exactly.

*Protégé*: So the best reinforcement is a living friend.

*Director*: A true friend, yes.

*Protégé*: And the more true friends we have, the better?

*Director*: I think so, at any rate.

*Protégé*: Does it dilute our friendship if we have too many friends?

*Director*: I haven't had that problem.

*Protégé*: And you have many friends.

*Director*: I have a few.

*Protégé*: I don't think it's possible to have many very good friends.

*Director*: Why not?

*Protégé*: There's only so much of us to go around. Don't you agree?

*Director*: You certainly have a point. I'm inclined to agree.

*Protégé*: So we have to choose our friends with care.

*Director*: And when we choose them, we must pursue them in earnest.

*Protégé*: That's why I'm going to lengths for the potential friend in my class.

*Director*: I thought you were going to lengths because you're shy.

*Protégé*: Do I seem shy to you?

*Director*: One-on-one with me? Hardly. But I wonder how you'll be when the three of us meet.

*Protégé*: You think I'll just shrink within and let you do all the talking?

*Director*: That's a risk, I think. But I know what to do.

*Protégé*: What will you do?

*Director*: Put questions to you so you have to speak.

*Protégé*: You'll put me on the spot?

*Director*: Not in the negative sense of that phrase. I'll gently encourage you. That's all. It'll be fine.

*Protégé*: I'm nervous about this. But I trust you.

*Director*: Good. I'll be your reinforcement as we talk. If you get into difficulties, I'll help you get out. But there is one thing I'm not sure I can help you with.

*Protégé*: What's that?

*Director*: Sometimes friends can stir violent emotions.

*Protégé*: You're afraid we'll stir him up?

*Director*: Not so much him.

*Protégé*: You're afraid I'll get stirred up?

*Director*: It often happens to the shy as they open up.

*Protégé*: What should I do if I do get stirred up?

*Director*: We'll have to talk you through it somehow.

*Protégé*: That sounds good—but how?

*Director*: Maybe I'll tell your friend about gentle summer breezes. Maybe that will remind you of what you said about that today.

*Protégé*: And if that doesn't work?

*Director*: We'll talk about the dangers of a typhoon.

*Protégé*: And if that fails?

*Director*: We need a fallback plan. I know. I can pretend I forgot about something for work that urgently needs to be done. I'll excuse myself. And you'll need to come with me because I drove you to school.

*Protégé*: That sounds good. But how will you know when it's time to execute the plan?

*Director*: I'll work the word hurricane into a sentence. If you're feeling okay and want to continue, just make eye contact with me and subtly shake your head no. If you're not doing well, make eye contact and nod your head yes, yes we should go.

*Protégé*: What if I'm so worked up I don't even make eye contact?

*Director*: I'll take that as a sign to make our escape.

### ~ Escape

*Director*. And then we'll do it again the following week, if you're still up for it.

*Protégé*: I think I will be. Thanks for working this out for me.

*Director*: Of course. It will be an adventure. And who knows what I'll learn?

*Protégé*: It's also a nice escape from work, isn't it?

*Director*: You're right about that.

*Protégé*: Is there violence at work?

*Director*: It's a regular gladiator show.

*Protégé*: It's really that bad?

*Director*: In violence against reason? Oh yes, it certainly is.

*Protégé*: What makes it so bad?

*Director*: Ambition and fear.

*Protégé*: In the same person?

*Director*: Sometimes, yes. But basically there are two classes of people at work. Those with ambition; and those who fear them. Neither is a great friend to reason.

*Protégé*: What's wrong with ambition?

*Director*: You're right to ask. Not all ambition is bad. Some ambition is very good. The ambition I see, however, involves tunnel vision on the prize. This can make people cruel. The others see this and they're afraid.

*Protégé*: Tunnel vision cuts you off from seeing reason.

*Director*: Yes. But it's easy to be fooled into thinking otherwise. Tunnel vision can produce lots of reasons, reasons backed by solid logic. But you never get the whole picture there.

*Protégé*: And if you're afraid of the ones with tunnel vision, you can't see reason either.

*Director*: You can't because you're like a poor rabbit, tensed and waiting for the attack. No one can reason in that frame of mind.

*Protégé*: Then why don't the rabbits escape? Get another job?

*Director*: Because most places are dominated by ambition and fear.

*Protégé*: Most but not all.

*Director*: That's right.

*Protégé*: Then why don't you go to one of those places?

*Director*: Because I'm needed here.

*Protégé*: By the rabbits?

*Director*: I help the rabbits when I can. But no, that's not the reason.

*Protégé*: Then what is?

*Director*: There are other people—not many, but some. I have business with them.

*Protégé*: Unfinished business?

*Director*: The business usually finishes when they leave the company.

*Protégé*: You want them to go?

*Director*: Yes, to one of those better places.

*Protégé*: What makes these places different? How do they exist?

*Director*: These other companies? That's a good question. They're in competition with the tunnel vision firms. How do they compete? The answer is simple. They act as one. But do you want to know how this is possible?

*Protégé*: I do.

*Director*: Nowhere in management is there someone with tunnel vision. If one appears, the others have to attack him or her with no mercy and drive them out. But there's another point.

*Protégé*: I want to hear it.

*Director*: Nowhere in management is there a rabbit.

*Protégé*: I like rabbits.

*Director*: So do I. But not this kind of rabbit in that kind of place.

*Protégé*: Are there rabbits outside of management?

*Director*: Usually some, but not many. Too many rabbits and you can't compete.

*Protégé*: Wouldn't you rather be in a place like this?

*Director*: No, I wouldn't.

*Protégé*: Not even if you finished all your business where you are now?

*Director*: Not even then.


~ ONE


*Protégé*: Why?

*Director*: That's not where I thrive.

*Protégé*: You thrive in the arena?

*Director*: Yes. I know my part. I'm meant to protect the possibility of a reasoned life. So I go to where it's under attack.

*Protégé*: And those others you spoke of, they go off and live a reasoned life?

*Director*: No one is perfect. But they go to a place where they can enjoy the reason they have.

*Protégé*: But peaceful enjoyment of reason isn't enough.

*Director*: It isn't? Why not?

*Protégé*: Is it enough for you? Or do you enjoy the fight?

*Director*: I enjoy the fight.

*Protégé*: And here I was thinking reason is gentle.

*Director*: But it is.

*Protégé*: Then how can it fight?

*Director*: I'm using our distinction—reason versus reasons. I fight with reasons, not reason itself. I save reason for my friends.

*Protégé*: But we should use reason, gentle reason, even in the face of violence.

*Director*: There are different levels of violence. In cases of extreme violence we have to fight fire with fire or worse.

*Protégé*: And you protect your friends this way?

*Director*: And myself, yes.

*Protégé*: Tell me something, *Director*. When we fight with reasons, is there a risk we might do violence to ourselves?

*Director*: Your instinct here is excellent. There's a very great risk.

*Protégé*: How do you avoid doing violence to yourself?

*Director*: You won't believe me if I tell you.

*Protégé*: You have to tell me.

*Director*: I have a gift.

*Protégé*: That's it? That's all you'll say? Then answer this. Is it also a curse?

*Director*: Anyone with a gift knows it can also be a curse. I think you know very well what I mean.

*Protégé*: I do.

*Director*: Good. So let's curse the curse and enjoy the gift.

*Protégé*: What happens if your friends at work, the others, try to copy you and it's not their gift?

*Director*: That's difficult. I have to encourage them to find their own way.

*Protégé*: A way away from you?

*Director*: Yes.

*Protégé*: And so you have to say goodbye? That must be hard.

*Director*: It is. And it would be too hard to bear if I didn't have hope.

*Protégé*: Hope for what?

*Director*: I need to explain. There are countless manifestations of reason. But at its core, reason is always one. To the extent friends keep in touch with the core, they are always together. I hope my friends and I will always be in touch with the core. Does that make any sense to you?

*Protégé*: Does it? Of course! I think I know exactly what you mean.

*Director*: So if things don't work out with your friend, but we see he's in touch with reason, you'll always have that in common with him. There is nothing more intimate or real.

*Protégé*: It's funny, but that takes off a lot of the pressure.

*Director*: Good! That's as it should be.

*Protégé*: But, *Director*, I have yet to meet anyone but you who's in touch with the core.

*Director*: Have you been looking?

*Protégé*: Honestly? Not with a plan. I'm just going from person to person randomly in life.

*Director*: I think you need a plan. This move we're making with your potential friend, that's according to a plan. But we may need something more.

*Protégé*: What?

*Director*: Criteria for selection.

*Protégé*: I agree. What criteria should we use?

*Director*: Well, maybe it's a sole criterion.

*Protégé*: Just one? What is it?

*Director*: Love.


~ LOVE


*Protégé*: Oh, don't tease.

*Director*: I'm serious. And I'm not talking about romantic love. I'm talking about a deep, human love.

*Protégé*: Like brotherly love?

*Director*: Yes, exactly like that. If you love someone, you want them to reach the core. And if they are already at the core, you want them to share what they think and know.

*Protégé*: I couldn't agree more.

*Director*: Do you often feel love?

*Protégé*: I do. But I don't think I'm in love with the right people.

*Director*: Why not?

*Protégé*: They hardly seem to be in touch with the core.

*Director*: How do you know? Are they violent with you?

*Protégé*: No.

*Director*: Are they violent with others?

*Protégé*: Not that I'm aware.

*Director*: Then what's the problem?

*Protégé*: They're not very... intellectual.

*Director*: Ah, I see. But there's a thing you should know.

*Protégé*: What?

*Director*: Sweet reason and intellectualism rarely go together in full. It's like the tunnel-visioned ambitious wolves. Intellectuals are often so focused on -isms that they lose sight of beautiful reason. Surely you've noticed this at school.

*Protégé*: I have. So where do I look for love?

*Director*: First, you have to remember not to rush into things. You need to feel your way in. Check for good signs along the way.

*Protégé*: And if the signs are bad?

*Director*: You break things off.

*Protégé*: I'm not good at that.

*Director*: What are you? A ship with barnacles attached? Scrape them off.

*Protégé*: But they'll take offense!

*Director*: And the offended will do violence to you?

*Protégé*: I'm afraid of what they'll say.

*Director*: What will they say? You're weird?

*Protégé*: How did you know?

*Director*: Know what?

*Protégé*: My fear.

*Director*: Everyone who knows reason knows that fear.

*Protégé*: Because reason is never the norm?

*Director*: That's part of it, yes. But it's mainly because reason itself is weird.


~ WEIRD


*Protégé*: What's weird about reason?

*Director*: What does weird mean?

*Protégé*: Here, I'll look it up. It says weird suggests the supernatural or the uncanny.

*Director*: Let's focus on the uncanny. Do you know what that word means?

*Protégé*: The uncanny is unsettling.

*Director*: That's the definition I use. Well, reason certainly can be unsettling, don't you think?

*Protégé*: Not if you're used to it.

*Director*: But do we ever really get used to reason?

*Protégé*: Why wouldn't we?

*Director*: Because reason is alive. It's never the same old reason.

*Protégé*: Alive? I can see how that might be unsettling.

*Director*: And if it's unsettling, might that not explain why people often react violently toward it?

*Protégé*: I think it might. But love is that way, too. Love is weird, unsettling.

*Director*: And that doesn't make love bad?

*Protégé*: Of course it doesn't!

*Director*: It wouldn't be better to settle?

*Protégé*: As in settle for something?

*Director*: 'Settle' has different senses. But you're on to something here. Reason won't let us settle; love won't let us settle—in your sense, and maybe in mine. They both expect we'll go for something more.

*Protégé*: I agree. But what about those lovers who settle together into a comfortable life?

*Director*: There's nothing wrong with comfort, is there?

*Protégé*: No, but then what's the something more?

*Director*: Who can say what goes on between two lovers? There might be something more that we can't see.

*Protégé*: And what about reason? Can we settle into a comfortable life with it?

*Director*: This is a key question. If the answer is no, many will want nothing to do with reason.

*Protégé*: Is the answer no?

*Director*: Yes.

*Protégé*: Why?

*Director*: Reason is not about comfort.

*Protégé*: And that's why we can only take it in relatively small doses?

*Director*: Exactly so.

*Protégé*: And when we do, we have to treat it with respect.

*Director*: Why?

*Protégé*: Because it's immensely powerful, if quiet and gentle.

*Director*: I don't know, *Protégé*. I don't think reason wants our respect.

*Protégé*: The respect is for our sake, in order to protect ourselves.

*Director*: From reason?

*Protégé*: From being overwhelmed.

*Director*: You may have a point. But I think it's best to simply listen and see. Respect might get in the way. Does that make any sense?

*Protégé*: I need to think about it more. It's part of the weirdness, isn't it?

*Director*: It certainly is. Reason, at the core, is beyond any precaution we might take. We should just listen and look carefully at what there is to hear and see.

*Protégé*: What's the worst reason can do to us?

*Director*: We do it to ourselves. We look and listen for a while, then decide we know all we need to know. We go off half-baked, half-cocked, or what have you. When we do, we work harm to ourselves and others.

*Protégé*: Is no reason better than some?

*Director*: That's a very difficult question to answer. Think of our friends the animals. Do they know reason?

*Protégé*: I don't know.

*Director*: Neither do I. They might be completely oblivious to it; or they might know it better than any of us could ever dream.

*Protégé*: I see why this is difficult. Some would say science separates us from the animals. But they seem to do just fine without it. My cat, as far as I can tell, is as happy as happy can be.

*Director*: I often think the same of mine. But it's hard to tell. Maybe they're good actors.

*Protégé*: Or maybe they're happy around us and miserable the rest of the time.

*Director*: I don't like to think that. But I take your point. Then again, we're talking about domesticated animals. Maybe they're different in the wild.

*Protégé*: Right. We just don't know.

### ~ Knowing

*Director*: In the end, what can we know?

*Protégé*: About animals?

*Director*: Yes, but also about other important things.

*Protégé*: Like violence and reason.

*Director*: Right.

*Protégé*: Well, as we said, we don't know if animals have reason. But we do know they do violence to one another on occasion.

*Director*: The term cat fight comes to mind.

*Protégé*: Yes.

*Director*: But what about violence itself. Do we always know it's there?

*Protégé*: Not always, no.

*Director*: But we know what violence is?

*Protégé*: We do.

*Director*: Can we know it if only we can see it?

*Protégé*: Or feel it, yes.

*Director*: What about reason? Do we know it when we see it or feel it?

*Protégé*: Of course, assuming we ourselves are in touch with reason.

*Director*: Are the violent in touch with reason?

*Protégé*: No.

*Director*: So the violent don't know reason when they see it or feel it?

*Protégé*: They might suspect it's reason, but they really don't know.

*Director*: Do the violent know they're violent?

*Protégé*: I often wonder that myself.

*Director*: But we, we can know they're violent.

*Protégé*: Of course.

*Director*: Can we know where violence comes from?

*Protégé*: That's what we've been talking about.

*Director*: Have we achieved a full understanding?

*Protégé*: No.

*Director*: What about reason? Have we achieved a full understanding of where it comes from?

*Protégé*: We have some vague notion of a core of reason. But no, we don't have a full understanding of where reason comes from. And I don't think we ever will.

*Director*: Why not?

*Protégé*: We're saying reason is weird. The weird defies full understanding. If we understood it, it wouldn't be weird. And then we have the added trouble.

*Director*: What trouble?

*Protégé*: We're distracted by 'reasons'.

*Director*: Ah, a very good point. But surely we know some things about reason.

*Protégé*: Well, we know it's always gentle.

*Director*: And?

*Protégé*: We know it's always sweet.

*Director*: Anything else?

*Protégé*: It can turn our world upside down. We have to be prepared for that.

*Director*: The fact that you know that suggests you're prepared.

*Protégé*: I hope I am.

*Director*: Is having your world turned upside down a gentle thing?

*Protégé*: I think it can be, if it's done the right way.

*Director*: Is it sweet?

*Protégé*: If your world was wrong side up? It can be sweet.

*Director*: I really am impressed. You seem so well prepared.

*Protégé*: For having my world turned upside down? Are you telling me in a delicate way I'm wrong side up?

*Director*: No, I'm not. But I'll tell you this. My world still gets turned upside down from time to time. I guess it just comes with the turf.


### ~ Rarity


*Protégé*: Some of my professors have turf.

*Director*: What do you mean?

*Protégé*: They're territorial with their knowledge.

*Director*: But I thought the whole point is to share that knowledge. That's what students are paying for, after all. No?

*Protégé*: Oh, they share. But heaven forbid anyone try to question that knowledge in a serious way.

*Director*: But questioning is one of the skills students pay to learn.

*Protégé*: Yes, but there are questions, and then there are questions.

*Director*: What's the difference between the two?

*Protégé*: Prestige.

*Director*: I don't understand.

*Protégé*: A question that upholds the prestige of the professor is accepted. A question that challenges that prestige is not greeted as warmly.

*Director*: What good is prestige?

*Protégé*: They say you can't eat it.

*Director*: That's true. What can you do with it?

*Protégé*: I really don't know what good it does.

*Director*: Would you turn it down?

*Protégé*: I would never even have the opportunity to do that.

*Director*: Why not?

*Protégé*: I don't care how I look in others' eyes.

*Director*: Not even those you love?

*Protégé*: Well, of course I care about that. But I don't want prestige from them.

*Director*: What do you want?

*Protégé*: Knowledge.

*Director*: What kind of knowledge?

*Protégé*: Knowledge that they love me back.

*Director*: Ah, you want the rarest knowledge there is.

*Protégé*: That's right.

*Director*: Did you know....

*Protégé*: Know what?

*Director*: Nothing.

*Protégé*: Don't do that. What?

*Director*: Alright. Did you know there will be times when violence can be done to that knowledge?

*Protégé*: I didn't know knowledge was a potential target.

*Director*: Oh, yes. More often than I care to think.

*Protégé*: How?

*Director*: You need to know something about knowledge. Knowledge is something we have to hold on to.

*Protégé*: Let me guess. Others will try to pry it away.

*Director*: Yes. So you have to hold on tight—to the knowledge.

*Protégé*: Why do you qualify it like that?

*Director*: Because we have to hold on to those we love—loosely.

*Protégé*: Even I know that. We must not be a source of violence ourselves by holding on too tight.

*Director*: Yes. This sort of violence comes from insecurities and sometimes paranoia.

*Protégé*: I wouldn't have put paranoia and violence together.

*Director*: Paranoia is generally accompanied by strong emotions.

*Protégé*: Jealousy.

*Director*: For one, yes. Jealousy is a violent emotion that works harm to knowledge. Can you see how this is?

*Protégé*: I can.

*Director*: A life truly free of jealousy, in whatever guise, is rare.

*Protégé*: Are philosophers free of jealousy?

*Director*: True philosophers? Yes.

*Protégé*: I want to be a true philosopher.

*Director*: You have the makings of one. But there's much to do.

*Protégé*: I know.

*Director*: Tell me. And be very honest here. Do you seek prestige from philosophy?

*Protégé*: I.... Maybe. But I know that's wrong.

*Director*: How do you know it's wrong?

*Protégé*: Because prestige distracts you from knowledge.

*Director*: The fact that you can see this at your age bodes well.

*Protégé*: What kind of knowledge do philosophers need?

*Director*: The kind that affects their reasoned lives.

*Protégé*: Nothing more?

*Director*: And nothing less.


~ Becoming


*Director*: But now I'm afraid.

*Protégé*: Of what?

*Director*: I'm afraid for you.

*Protégé*: Why would you be afraid for me? I intend to spend my time tucked safely away in the library.

*Director*: More violence is directed against potential philosophers than anyone else.

*Protégé*: Than anyone else?

*Director*: Yes.

*Protégé*: I don't understand. Why?

*Director*: Because they're a threat.

*Protégé*: To what?

*Director*: To things the violent believe.

*Protégé*: What's the greatest thing they believe?

*Director*: It's something they're sure they know.

*Protégé*: What?

*Director*: That violence will stifle philosophy's growth.

*Protégé*: Will it?

*Director*: It certainly can.

*Protégé*: How do we prevent that from happening?

*Director*: Each situation is unique.

*Protégé*: You can't tell me what I need to do?

*Director*: No, I can't.

*Protégé*: How does that make you feel?

*Director*: Me? Better that you asked this and not something else. It's a good sign.

*Protégé*: Why?

*Director*: Because knowing you'll have to figure it out yourself doesn't paralyze you—and you still have concern for others, for me. That's very becoming in a philosopher, you know.

*Protégé*: What else is becoming in a philosopher?

*Director*: The courage to ask.

*Protégé*: Ask what?

*Director*: More about what everyone believes.

*Protégé*: I'm confused. What am I asking about? What all people believe? Or what each individual believes?

*Director*: Both. 'All people' today is comprised of many an 'individual'.

*Protégé*: I read a philosopher once who talked about how we think we're individuals but we're really all the same. Most of us, anyway.

*Director*: The Ancient Greeks had no truck with our notion of 'individuals'.

*Protégé*: That's because they simply were individuals, some of them at least. They didn't even have to try.

*Director*: I'm not sure about that. But I am sure that many of us, in this, our land of individualism, try hard to differentiate ourselves.

*Protégé*: Yes, and it all comes back to violence.

*Director*: Tell me more.

*Protégé*: Those who strive hardest to be an 'individual' do violence to those around them.

*Director*: How so?

*Protégé*: They want those around them to see them as other than they are.

*Director*: What are they?

*Protégé*: The same as everyone else.

*Director*: Hmm. So you're saying they force their self-image upon us?

*Protégé*: Exactly.

*Director*: But are we really all the same?

*Protégé*: What differentiates us?

*Director*: Well, true differentiation, it seems to me, comes from not caring a whit what others think we are.

*Protégé*: And in our land most everyone cares what others think.

*Director*: Yes. Not to care is rare, and most becoming.


~ MONSTERS


*Director*: But now I'm not so sure. Have you ever heard it said that monsters don't care what others think or believe?

*Protégé*: I have. But I see it another way.

*Director*: How do you see it?

*Protégé*: The real monsters are those who think you should care.

*Director*: Yes. But what do you say if they tell you they just want you to be prudent? And before you answer, I'll note that the young are typically less prudent than the old.

*Protégé*: I'll always side with the young.

*Director*: Even if it goes against your interests?

*Protégé*: *Director*, my interests are with the young. If I'm overly prudent I do violence to myself and them.

*Director*: Spoken like a philosopher.

*Protégé*: Like a philosopher? Or as a philosopher?

*Director*: It's too early to say.

*Protégé*: How do I prove myself?

*Director*: By feeling no need to prove yourself.

*Protégé*: How do I get to that point?

*Director*: By proving yourself to yourself.

*Protégé*: As distinct from proving myself to others?

*Director*: Precisely.

*Protégé*: But what if I can only prove myself to myself by proving myself to others?

*Director*: Then you're a poor old monstrosity.

*Protégé*: That's rather harsh.

*Director*: But it's also rather true.

*Protégé*: How can I prove myself to myself?

*Director*: You can overcome violent attacks.

*Protégé*: But won't that prove something to those who attack?

*Director*: It might merely prove you're strange.

*Protégé*: Why strange?

*Director*: Because to them, the monsters who attack, there's no understanding why you're able to stand up tall in the face of their worst.

*Protégé*: It helps that I know what they want.

*Director*: What do they want?

*Protégé*: For me to join in.

*Director*: In doing violence to yourself?

*Protégé*: Yes. And to them. They expect no less. And when they don't get it? I'm strange.

*Director*: Monsters look for mutual abuse. Is that what you're saying?

*Protégé*: It is. Am I right?

*Director*: I'm learning from you. And yes, I think you're right. But tell me. What's the opposite of a monster?

*Protégé*: Do you want me to say it's an angel?

*Director*: No, I'm looking for something more human.

*Protégé*: But you already have your answer. The opposite of a monster is a human being, simple and full.

*Director*: What does full humanity take?

*Protégé*: Kindness.

*Director*: To all?

*Protégé*: To those like ourselves.

~ KINDNESS

*Director*: Kindness is the opposite of violence, no?

*Protégé*: Yes.

*Director*: And we don't show kindness to monsters.

*Protégé*: Positively not.

*Director*: Why?

*Protégé*: Because kindness takes effort and it's wasted on them.

*Director*: Kindness takes effort?

*Protégé*: On monsters it does.

*Director*: I take your point. But kindness to the kind?

*Protégé*: That's as effortless as can be. A gentle summer breeze.

*Director*: I agree. So we're saying it's foolish to waste effort on the violent.

*Protégé*: We are.

*Director*: But haven't you ever heard the phrase 'kill them with kindness'?

*Protégé*: I don't know how I feel about that. Sometimes I'd rather it were just 'kill them'—and leave it at that.

*Director*: Can kindness kill?

*Protégé*: I don't see how. It might frustrate or annoy. But kill? A monster? I'm not sure how.

*Director*: What should we do with violent monsters?

*Protégé*: Put them to death.

*Director*: Literally?

*Protégé*: Well this begs the question. We've been talking about violence. And mostly we've been talking about violence to thought, or the mind, or knowledge, or soul—whatever. But if we talk about violence to the body, the rest of the body, the flesh, to the point where we die—then we should put them to literal death.

*Director*: What if there's reason to hope one day they'll change, see reason, come to the light of day?

*Protégé*: They've forfeited their right to that chance.

*Director*: What if they commit a lesser offense and they change?

*Protégé*: Have you ever known someone to make this change?

*Director*: I haven't. But I have known people who've grown old.

*Protégé*: What do you mean?

*Director*: As they lose their strength, people often change their tune.

*Protégé*: I've seen that firsthand.

*Director*: So what do you think? Should we forgive them because they sing a different tune?

*Protégé*: No, I don't think so.

*Director*: Spoken like someone who's had violence done to him.

*Protégé*: Have you?

*Director*: I have.

*Protégé*: Do you think you could forgive the brute who did it to you?

*Director*: If I see they're truly in touch with reason? I like to think the answer is yes.


~ BRUTES AND DEVILS


*Protégé*: Why do you think people grow brutish?

*Director*: It's hard to say. But I'll say this. I think their light was extinguished at some point. Sometimes very young; sometimes at an older age. But it's clear to me the light is out.

*Protégé*: You can see it in their eyes. They're dead.

*Director*: Yes. But there's a difference between brutes and devils.

*Protégé*: What's the difference?

*Director*: Devils have a wicked glint in their eye.

*Protégé*: 'Glint' as distinct from 'light'?

*Director*: Certainly. Light comes from within. A glint is a reflection from without. Or so I like to define these things.

*Protégé*: Your definitions make sense to me. But the devils, where do they find that light? In the eyes of others?

*Director*: I've asked myself where the light comes from many times. I have yet to find the answer.

*Protégé*: Maybe it's that they light human beings afire, and revel in the blaze.

*Director*: You may be right. They warm their cold souls this way.

*Protégé*: They rub their icy hands together in glee.

*Director*: So much for devils. But what do they deserve?

*Protégé*: For a capital offense? Death.

*Director*: And brutes?

*Protégé*: The same. But are we saying brutes become devils if they step in front of the flame?

*Director*: That's an interesting question. Is there a difference to be seen in their eyes?

*Protégé*: Devils show more intelligence.

*Director*: Who deserves more punishment? The intelligent?

*Protégé*: I think it should be the same.

*Director*: Greater talent doesn't deserve greater punishment or leniency?

*Protégé*: Death is death.

*Director*: But what about torture?

*Protégé*: No, then we're like them.

*Director*: Alright. I had to check.

*Protégé*: I just want them out of the way.

*Director*: What if, short of killing them, we could put them on a different way?

*Protégé*: One that leaves our way clear?

*Director*: Yes. What if we could make them our slaves?

*Protégé*: I have to admit, I'm partial to this idea. How?

*Director*: Kind human beings would have to unite. And we couldn't be cruel to our slaves. We would simply treat them as... slaves.

*Protégé*: But isn't slavery inherently cruel? The kind can never be cruel. A quick and painless death would be best.

*Director*: But I thought you were partial to my idea.

*Protégé*: Sometimes we want what we shouldn't.

*Director*: And brutes and devils?

*Protégé*: They know no shoulds.

*Director*: I believe you that brutes know no shoulds. But I think devils know them all too well.

*Protégé*: Yes, but they ignore them with abandon.

~ SHOULD

*Director*: But there's something about 'should'.

*Protégé*: What is it?

*Director*: Do you think it does violence to 'want'?

*Protégé*: Want as in desire? No! Want is more likely to do violence to should.

*Director*: What's a troublesome want?

*Protégé*: I want to eat ice cream three meals a day. But I shouldn't.

*Director*: Why not?

*Protégé*: My health will eventually suffer.

*Director*: You're sure about this?

*Protégé*: Pretty sure.

*Director*: Have you ever done violence to this should?

*Protégé*: I have.

*Director*: And yet the should is still strong?

*Protégé*: Not as strong as it should be.

*Director*: Should should be strong?

*Protégé*: If it's a true should? Yes, of course.

*Director*: And a strong should does violence to your dream of three pints a day.

*Protégé*: Well, now you're changing things up.

*Director*: How so?

*Protégé*: We spoke of violence to a want. Now you're speaking of violence to a dream.

*Director*: Is one more real than the other?

*Protégé*: No, but the former is more demanding.

*Director*: Maybe you haven't had the right dream.

*Protégé*: Maybe.

*Director*: Can we do away with wants?

*Protégé*: How would we?

*Director*: Reason with them.

*Protégé*: No, I think that rarely works.

*Director*: And what about dreams? Can we reason a dream away?

*Protégé*: We analyze the dream, using gentle reason?

*Director*: Yes.

*Protégé*: This might work for some dreams, sure. But remind me why we're trying to get rid of our dreams?

*Director*: We only would when they are in conflict with a reasoned should.

*Protégé*: The should is the end of the reasoning? The should must become an 'is'?

*Director*: When should is an is, things are good. No?

*Protégé*: Yes.

*Director*: Tell me something. Does it matter where the should comes from?

*Protégé*: What, you mean from inside or without? As long as it comes from reason, it shouldn't matter.

*Director*: If someone forces a should on you, is that violence?

*Protégé*: It is.

*Director*: What if it's a parent forcing you to eat your vegetables? Violence?

*Protégé*: I want to say yes.

*Director*: Then you should say yes.

*Protégé*: Yes. But there's something good about this violence.

*Director*: I was wondering if we'd come to that.

*Protégé*: The violence is for our own good.

*Director*: But not all violence is for our own good.

*Protégé*: Of course not. The trick is being able to judge when the violent are telling the truth, or when they're telling lies.

*Director*: Hmm.

*Protégé*: What is it?

*Director*: There's another difficulty here. What if the violent truly believe their should is for your own good?

*Protégé*: And it's not?

*Director*: Yes.

*Protégé*: We urgently need to know our own good.

*Director*: I wholeheartedly agree.

*Protégé*: But children don't know their own good.

*Director*: I suppose it depends on the child, and the circumstances they're in.

## ~ GOOD

*Director*: It all comes down to listening to reason.

*Protégé*: Sure, but don't we have to come of age in order to listen?

*Director*: Yes, but coming of age just means you've begun to listen. When did you start listening to reason?

*Protégé*: I don't know exactly. I suppose I always did, as far back as I can remember. But now I wonder.

*Director*: What do you wonder?

*Protégé*: What if you can say something like this? 'This is when I started listening to reason—when I was twenty-four years old.' Do you think there are people like that?

*Director*: I know full well there are. Do you think you're better than them?

*Protégé*: No!

*Director*: Are you lying to me?

*Protégé*: No, I'm not. You can listen to reason and be a coward who doesn't act on the reason you hear. The man at twenty-four might have started late but have more courage than someone like me.

*Director*: Okay. But let's get back to our point. We listen to reason in order to know our own good. True?

*Protégé*: True.

*Director*: Is that the only reason to listen to reason?

*Protégé*: Well, we might want to know others' good, too.

*Director*: I see. Then tell me. When we know another's good, what do we have to do?

*Protégé*: Tell them about it.

*Director*: And that's our good? The telling?

*Protégé*: No, our good is when they act on their good.

*Director*: How so?

*Protégé*: Then they're happier. And when you're happier, you make a better friend.

*Director*: It's good to have friends.

*Protégé*: Is there any doubt?

*Director*: Well....

*Protégé*: Tell me.

*Director*: It's just a little doubt I have. What if our friend draws fire?

*Protégé*: You mean what if they're a target of violent attack?

*Director*: Yes. What if their good is to provoke?

*Protégé*: Is that really anyone's good?

*Director*: I can imagine times when it is.

*Protégé*: And you're wondering if we can be guilty, so to speak, by association—and come under attack ourselves.

*Director*: Yes. What do you think?

*Protégé*: If we give the friendship up out of fear, we're cowards.

*Director*: What if it's not out of fear?

*Protégé*: What would it be out of?

*Director*: Prudence.

*Protégé*: Prudence is often a sort of fear.

*Director*: That's true. Then I think there are only two ways about it. If we're strong enough, we stand by our friend.

*Protégé*: And if we're not?

*Director*: The friend, as a friend, will understand. That's what's good about friends.


~ SHAME


*Protégé*: How do we not feel shame if we know we're too weak?

*Director*: We have to let our knowledge of our other strengths sustain us.

*Protégé*: I'm not sure I could.

*Director*: You'd have to, *Protégé*. Otherwise you'd do violence to yourself.

*Protégé*: But shouldn't we be ashamed of our weakness? Won't that spur us to grow strong?

*Director*: Be very careful of spurs.

*Protégé*: Why?

*Director*: Because they work violence on us.

*Protégé*: Maybe we need a little violence to help us on our way.

*Director*: Better to persuade than spur.

*Protégé*: Always?

*Director*: If there's a choice? Always.

*Protégé*: So you admit there are times when we have no choice and have to let shame spur us on.

*Director*: Tell me something, *Protégé*. How does shame spur?

*Protégé*: It makes us feel we don't want to be what we are.

*Director*: Shame wants us to change.

*Protégé*: Yes.

*Director*: We've been talking of shame as if it were an internal thing. But don't others attempt to shame us, as well?

*Protégé*: Yes, and that can be a form of violence. We have to resist.

*Director*: What's a classic example of this sort of violent shame?

*Protégé*: Body shaming. Making you feel ashamed of how you are.

*Director*: Too short, too tall, to skinny, too fat?

*Protégé*: And so on, yes.

*Director*: Why do you think shamers try to shame us here?

*Protégé*: Hurt people hurt.

*Director*: What does that mean?

*Protégé*: They have been made to feel ashamed of themselves, and so they try to do the same to others.

*Director*: Is that always the case?

*Protégé*: What else could it be?

*Director*: Maybe they feel no shame. And this launches them on a sort of power trip where they trample on others.

*Protégé*: Are you saying we should make them feel shame in order to rein them in?

*Director*: That's not a business I'd like to be in.

*Protégé*: So what should we do?

*Director*: Ignore them.

*Protégé*: Ha! Easier said than done.

### ~ IGNORING

*Protégé*: It's awfully hard to ignore when violence is being done to you.

*Director*: I agree. But it has to be done in some cases. Look at me. What if someone makes fun of my face?

*Protégé*: Your face is fine.

*Director*: Thank you. But let's say someone makes fun of it. What do I need to know in order to ignore?

*Protégé*: You need to know your face is fine.

*Director*: Knowledge will save me here?

*Protégé*: Yes.

*Director*: But what if my face is really ugly? And they point this fact out? Should I be ashamed of the truth?

*Protégé*: Your face is your face no matter what anyone says.

*Director*: Yes, exactly so. But should I be ashamed?

*Protégé*: No.

*Director*: Why?

*Protégé*: Because it's not your fault.

*Director*: We should only be ashamed of things that are our fault?

*Protégé*: That's a good rule.

*Director*: Does shame like that harm?

*Protégé*: Only if we don't accept it as a prompt toward a cure.

*Director*: Shame as a prompt toward a cure. That's interesting. What if we ignore the prompt?

*Protégé*: That's what the shameless do.

*Director*: And they're never cured.

*Protégé*: Never.

*Director*: But do they really feel the prompt? I mean, we're saying they feel no shame.

*Protégé*: There's nothing to be done about the shameless.

*Director*: What's to be done about those who do feel shame but try to ignore it?

*Protégé*: It's like ignoring an itch. It only gets worse. At some point you have to scratch.

*Director*: Scratch the shame away. That sounds somehow violent.

*Protégé*: I think it is. And the scratching might well be a form of acting out against others.

*Director*: Violence to others scratches our shame?

*Protégé*: Yes, I think that's the way of it.

*Director*: And, to be sure, what's the nature of this violence?

*Protégé*: Shaming others to compensate for the shame you feel.

*Director*: Can we others ignore this violence?

*Protégé*: I guess it depends.

*Director*: On what?

*Protégé*: Whether we're confident enough in ourselves.

*Director*: How can we be that?

*Protégé*: We must know no shame.

*Director*: We must be shameless?

*Protégé*: Yes, but not in that sense.

*Director*: In what sense, then?

*Protégé*: In the sense of having done nothing that would cause us shame. So I'd say we're not shameless. We're without shame.


~ Pain


*Director*: If someone kicks us in the guts, it hurts. Yes?

*Protégé*: Literally kicks us in the guts? Of course.

*Director*: And it always hurts. There's nothing we can do.

*Protégé*: It hurts even the very strong, if only a little.

*Director*: But with intellectual or spiritual violence, we can do something about it. We can train ourselves not to feel it, not to feel the pain. Do you agree?

*Protégé*: I agree. But I'm not very far along in my training.

*Director*: We should open a gym to train for this sort of thing.

*Protégé*: Ha, ha! That would be great!

*Director*: Maybe we'll tell your potential friend about this gym and see what he thinks.

*Protégé*: Let's hold off on that until we know him better.

*Director*: Why? Are you embarrassed?

*Protégé*: It's just that it will sound...

*Director*: ...a little weird?

*Protégé*: Yes.

*Director*: But the weird attracts the weird. And reason, we said, is weird. Violence isn't weird. Violence just is.

*Protégé*: You have a point. But let's give it some time.

*Director*: Sounds like a plan. But let's fish around and see what sort of inner pain he might have, something that might attract him to the gym.

*Protégé*: Fishing for pain isn't something I think is good for our first get together.

*Director*: Well, let's see how things go. Maybe we'll have to wait until later, when we're deep into the verbs. Those verbs can be painful, you know.

*Protégé*: Oh, I know. So you think you're going to segue from one type of pain to the other?

*Director*: Maybe. Again, we'll see how things go.

*Protégé*: What other potential segues are there?

*Director*: There are many possibilities in any given conversation. I'll ask some general questions. Do you like school? What's your favorite class? What's your least favorite class? Where are you from? Do you like it here better? What don't you like about either place?

*Protégé*: You're just hoping somewhere along the line he expresses displeasure.

*Director*: Yes, and displeasure and pain are cousins.

*Protégé*: And both might stem from violence.

*Director*: If we can get him talking about violence, we can get him talking about the gym.

*Protégé*: Then we might create this gym.

*Director*: And invite others to join.

*Protégé*: What is this gym? Some sort of philosophical school?

*Director*: The school of pain? Why not?

*Protégé*: 'School of Pain' is an unlucky name. We need something that talks about resistance to violence.

*Director*: The Anti-Violence School?

*Protégé*: Sounds a little too weird. Maybe we don't give it a name. Maybe it's just the group of friends that meets for coffee once a week.

*Director*: Sounds good to me. But let's not limit it to violence. Let's talk all about reason.

*Protégé*: Okay. But I have a suspicion.

*Director*: What?

*Protégé*: Reason might not exist —if it weren't for violence.


~ REASON, AGAIN


*Director*: What makes you say that?

*Protégé*: Violence stirs us up. When we're stirred, we're more open to reason.

*Director*: You said reason might not exist. Why are you holding back? And what more, don't you think we have to be at peace to listen to reason? When we're all stirred up aren't we less likely to hear the quiet voice?

*Protégé*: Reason is a reaction to violence. It's a rebellion. Violence comes first. Reason follows in its wake, in order to explain what happened and decide how best to rebel.

*Director*: So without violence we're just happy little vegetables, growing in the earth?

*Protégé*: I don't know. Like I said, it's just a suspicion.

*Director*: Maybe there's truth in it. But in order to see that truth, we'd have to go back beyond reason and see if violence is always there. And, if possible, we need to go back beyond violence and see if anything else is there, just to be sure.

*Protégé*: How do we do that?

*Director*: We reason.

*Protégé*: But if we reason how can we get back beyond reason?

*Director*: Maybe there's no way for us to know. At least for now. Let's keep it all in mind and maybe someday things will be clear.

*Protégé*: Yes, that sounds good.

*Director*: But something remarkable has happened.

*Protégé*: What do you mean?

*Director*: We went from saying violence stems from a rebellion against reason, to suggesting reason arises from a reaction to violence.

*Protégé*: You're right. That is remarkable. But there's something I wonder.

*Director*: What is it?

*Protégé*: If we're going to rebel against violence, wouldn't our natural instinct be to rebel with violence?

*Director*: Fight fire with fire?

*Protégé*: Yes.

*Director*: Then why reason?

*Protégé*: Maybe we're overwhelmed, and don't have the level of violence it takes to rebel.

*Director*: So reason is some sort of act of desperation?

*Protégé*: That's what I'm wondering. What do you think?

*Director*: There might be some truth in that. I'll have to give it some thought.

*Protégé*: You haven't thought about this before?

*Director*: Not like this, no.

*Protégé*: You're learning something from me?

*Director*: Why do you seem surprised? I learn wherever I can. Oh, but I'm sorry. I didn't mean to imply that learning with you isn't special.

*Protégé*: Don't worry. In order to deflate you had to have been puffed up.

*Director*: Well, feel free to deflate me if ever I seem that way.

*Protégé*: I will—or at least I'll try.

*Director*: Why do you make it sound hard?

*Protégé*: Because if you puff up, you'll bristle with reasons!

*Director*: That's the worst sort of puffed up thing there is. So how would you deflate me?

*Protégé*: I'd pluck one of your bristles and use it against you.

*Director*: An excellent technique. But how would you use it against me?

*Protégé*: I'd use reason on your 'reason' until you were forced to succumb on this point. And once I drive this single point home, your other bristles won't matter. The damage will be done.

## ~ THE POINT

*Director*: You're teaching me a good lesson.

*Protégé*: How so?

*Director*: We need to concentrate on our point, not spread ourselves too thin across a great many points.

*Protégé*: Yes, all the force should be behind one. If we can puncture the surface with that, we've won.

*Director*: That's all it takes?

*Protégé*: Just one, yes. Then the rest really don't matter.

*Director*: Can it be just any point?

*Protégé*: I think it can. Why, would you choose some special point?

*Director*: I would fight the enemy on what philosophy is.

*Protégé*: And if they don't care what philosophy is?

*Director*: Then we have to find something they care about. That's where we have good effect.

*Protégé*: It's best if we can figure out what's in their heart of hearts.

*Director*: You'd go straight for the heart?

*Protégé*: Of course. Wouldn't you?

*Director*: I would. I just didn't know how ruthless you could be.

*Protégé*: Do you think it's bad?

*Director*: To the contrary. Ruthlessness here is good. But as you press your point, your attack, expect attack in return.

*Protégé*: I know. They'll find my weak point and press with all their might.

*Director*: What's your weak point?

*Protégé*: My body. I'm frail, in case you hadn't noticed.

*Director*: They'll make fun of you?

*Protégé*: Yes, and push me around.

*Director*: Two types of violence at once. Hmm. Then never let them get you alone. Always be in places where the worst they can do is with words.

*Protégé*: What will I do? Walk to class with an escort of friends?

*Director*: If you can arrange it? Yes. Do what you must.

*Protégé*: Alright. But what's their weak point?

*Director*: That they have nothing better to do.

*Protégé*: I think that's true. But it hardly hits home, if you know what I mean.

*Director*: I think we have to find someone attractive to them to make this attack.

*Protégé*: That would hit home. But finding someone able and willing will be hard.


## ~ ATTRACTION


*Director*: Let's come at this from a different angle. Can attraction do violence to the soul?

*Protégé*: That's a hard question.

*Director*: Why?

*Protégé*: Because to answer it we'd have to know what attraction is, and what is the soul.

*Director*: Spoken like a philosopher.

*Protégé*: Again only like a philosopher? Not as a philosopher?

*Director*: Answer this, philosopher. Can we ever be attracted to the wrong thing?

*Protégé*: I think that happens all the time.

*Director*: Like moths to the flame?

*Protégé*: Like that, yes.

*Director*: Then we need to find the equivalent of a flame for the enemy to destroy themselves upon. Tell me, and maybe this will help us find it. What does the enemy want of their attraction?

*Protégé*: Satisfaction.

*Director*: Physical satisfaction?

*Protégé*: Usually, yes.

*Director*: What other satisfaction is there?

*Protégé*: Mental satisfaction.

*Director*: What does that involve?

*Protégé*: Breaking the other.

*Director*: Is that a reasoned satisfaction? You said it was mental.

*Protégé*: Maybe it's not mental.

*Director*: What is it then?

*Protégé*: The delight of a twisted soul.

*Director*: What twists a soul?

*Protégé*: Violence done to it.

*Director*: What about the violence it does?

*Protégé*: An excellent point. That, too.

*Director*: To put it in so many words—violence twists the soul. So what happens when this twisted soul approaches the flame?

*Protégé*: It all depends on how open they are.

*Director*: What do you mean?

*Protégé*: How loose. Haven't you heard that drunks don't get hurt in car crashes because they're so loose? The ones who don't open up, don't stay loose—they get hurt.

*Director*: Attraction involves a sort of crash?

*Protégé*: Yes, I think that describes it well.

*Director*: But what if your car crash example is just an urban myth?

*Protégé*: Myths have their root in truth, more often than not.

*Director*: So you want your enemies sober for the crash.

*Protégé*: That sounds funny to say, but I think it's true.

*Director*: Maybe the attraction will sober them up.

*Protégé*: I hope so.

*Director*: What makes them drunk?

*Protégé*: Doing violence to others—whatever sort of violence. They get drunk on that.

*Director*: What do you get drunk on?

*Protégé*: Me? I'm not sure I get drunk. What about you?

*Director*: Who, me? You think I'll say reason gets me drunk, don't you?

*Protégé*: I don't think anything. I just want to know.

*Director*: Is that what attracts you to me?

*Protégé*: What do you mean?

*Director*: That I don't make you think anything.

*Protégé*: Oh, stop. You do make me think.

*Director*: Then you're thinking about what makes me drunk. Tell me your suspicion.

*Protégé*: Alright. I suspect reason makes you drunk. But not like a typical drunkenness. Reason makes you feel good, but doesn't take away your judgment—or give you a hangover afterwards. That's what I suspect. So what do you say?

*Director*: Remember, we said reason is weird. It sometimes makes me feel good. It sometimes makes me feel... weird. And it does, Protégé, take away my judgment at times.

*Protégé*: Why?

*Director*: What is judgment?

*Protégé*: Knowing what's best to do.

*Director*: What if my knowledge of what's best to do is actually based on opinion, false opinion?

*Protégé*: You'd be right not to heed that judgment.

*Director*: Reason makes me see that judgment for what it is. So it makes me seem drunk, because I don't heed what people take to be my normal judgment.

*Protégé*: Or their normal judgment.

*Director*: True. There are some who think because we don't share their judgment, we lack judgment.

*Protégé*: And it's not just some.

*Director*: Do you think those of 'judgment' don't listen to reason?

*Protégé*: I think they listen to a sliver of reason, and lock it up with air tight logic.

*Director*: And they're only attracted to those with similar slivers?

*Protégé*: They side with them, yes. But attraction is something else. They're often attracted to others, others outside their sliver. And it's painful for them to be attracted there. So they want to do violence to stop the pain.

*Director*: Violence to themselves?

*Protégé*: Yes. They do violence to the attraction, to keep their air tight logic intact. But sometimes they do violence to the object of attraction. And that's very sad.


~ Logic


*Director*: Why does their air tight logic matter?

*Protégé*: It makes them feel safe.

*Director*: Safe against attraction?

*Protégé*: Mostly, yes.

*Director*: Safe against others who attack?

*Protégé*: I think they find solace here, too.

*Director*: And when they themselves attack?

*Protégé*: Their logic lends them strength.

*Director*: Against those who don't know them for what they really are?

*Protégé*: Yes. And I'll tell you, *Director*. Our talk is making me feel strength against them.

*Director*: That's good! Does that mean you'll employ logic against them?

*Protégé*: Broad ranging logic, yes.

*Director*: But what about focusing on that single point?

*Protégé*: Broad ranging logic narrows down to the single point—when employed by those who know.

*Director*: You're sounding more and more like a philosopher.

*Protégé*: That's what philosophers know?

*Director*: They know it all comes down to that single point.

*Protégé*: And when they carry that point?

*Director*: They hope the discussion opens enough to share reason itself.

*Protégé*: Logic isn't reason?

*Director*: Logic is logic. Reason is reason.

*Protégé*: How can you say that?

*Director*: Logic—generally speaking, as it's used today—isn't weird

*Protégé*: How can it be weird?

*Director*: It's weird when it operates on a fertile field.

*Protégé*: What's a fertile field?

*Director*: Somewhere where there can be life.

*Protégé*: Life is weird, isn't it?

*Director*: True life? It's very weird indeed.

*Protégé*: And people are afraid of the weird.

*Director*: That's why they lock their logic up and throw away the key.

*Protégé*: And here we philosophers come along with the key.

*Director*: Yes. It makes them want to do violence to us.

*Protégé*: I know that's true. So what's to be done?

*Director*: We can leave them with the key then slowly step away.

*Protégé*: It somehow doesn't seem fair.

*Director*: What doesn't seem fair?

*Protégé*: They want to do violence to us for giving them a wonderful gift—the key they threw away.

*Director*: Maybe we should leave a gift on everyone's door.

*Protégé*: That sounds nice. But why?

*Director*: Because we want them to see we don't mean it as harm. After all, they'll see we even give similar gifts to friends.

*Protégé*: You mean it? Give gifts to all?

*Director*: I do mean it. And yes.


~ GIFTS


*Protégé*: But to some the gift is a sort of bomb. And maybe to more than some.

*Director*: What can I say? That's the weirdness of reason. But the gift wouldn't be a bomb if it were met with reason. Reason has the power to disarm.

*Protégé*: What other powers does reason have?

*Director*: What would you like it to have?

*Protégé*: The power to change ourselves.

*Director*: To what?

*Protégé*: Philosophers.

*Director*: Ah. But the life of philosophy is hard—not what most people think of when they think of gifts.

*Protégé*: You seem to enjoy it.

*Director*: I enjoy hard things. Do you?

*Protégé*: Frail thing that I am?

*Director*: You, whatever you are.

*Protégé*: I think I might enjoy philosophy.

*Director*: Why?

*Protégé*: Because it repels violent attacks.

*Director*: And you have had your share of violent attacks.

*Protégé*: I have.

*Director*: Is that what philosophy is all about, repelling attacks? Or is it more about giving gifts of reason like Old Saint Nick?

*Protégé*: Philosophy is all about reason, whatever form it might take.

*Director*: A fine answer. But do you know what else philosophy sometimes involves?

*Protege*: Tell me.

*Director*: Violence, my friend. Violence.


### ~ BELIEFS


*Protégé*: I never expected that's what you'd say. What is philosophy violent toward?

*Director*: False beliefs.

*Protégé*: How?

*Director*: It seeks to disabuse people of them.

*Protégé*: It does violence to false beliefs?

*Director*: That's what it does.

*Protégé*: Through reason?

*Director*: For some it takes more than reason.

*Protégé*: And you're all too happy to comply. But name a false belief, so I can understand.

*Director*: You believe you're God's gift. Can you understand?

*Protégé*: Someone like that won't listen to reason, I'm sure. So the disabuse takes something more. And that's really what philosophy does?

*Director*: Your philosophy professors might not agree, but that's what this philosopher does.

*Protégé*: I want to do philosophy to you.

*Director*: Find a false belief and proceed.

*Protégé*: You believe I'm strong.

*Director*: No, friend, I don't. I know. I can see you're strong, though not in a way many might perceive.

*Protégé*: But that's always the way.

*Director*: What do you mean?

*Protégé*: I say you believe; you say you know.

*Director*: There's a close correspondence between belief and knowledge. But not when it comes to false belief.

*Protégé*: You believe philosophy makes you strong.

*Director*: No, I don't.

*Protégé*: You know philosophy makes you strong?

*Director*: No, I know philosophy makes me...

*Protégé*: ...weak?

*Director*: No, not weak. Philosophy is weird, suffice it to say.

*Protégé*: So philosophy makes you weird?

*Director*: Yes, I think that's true. But, and I'll only confess this to you—I try to hide my weirdness.

*Protégé*: From whom?

*Director*: Those who can't appreciate it for what it is.

*Protégé*: And what is it?

*Director*: The legitimate heir of reason.

*Protégé*: What makes weirdness legitimate?

*Director*: It bends to every one of reason's whims.

*Protégé*: That makes philosophy sound weak.

*Director*: I know what you mean. But bending to reason's whims is no easy thing. Can you see how?

*Protégé*: I can imagine how.

*Director*: Then imagine this. You have a cherished belief.

*Protégé*: What belief?

*Director*: It doesn't matter. But here, let's say this. You believe in a particular political philosophy. It guides much of your life. But one day you listen to reason and realize it's rot.

*Protégé*: That's good.

*Director*: Yes. But it's easy to say 'that's good'. Is it easy to live up to what you now know and learn a better way?

*Protégé*: No, I think that's very hard.

*Director*: Why do you think this is?

*Protégé*: Because we're reeling from the loss of our cherished belief.

*Director*: And when we're reeling we don't know where we are?

*Protégé*: We don't.

*Director*: And we don't know where to go?

*Protégé*: We have no idea.

*Director*: So what must we do?

*Protégé*: There's only one thing to be done. And you know what it is.

*Director*: Tell me all the same.

*Protégé*: We must strain to hear what reason says.


~ Experience


*Director*: You sound like you have experience here.

*Protégé*: I once believed in something bad.

*Director*: Did you cherish that belief?

*Protégé*: I did. I felt I had a great truth that few understood in full.

*Director*: What did you believe?

*Protégé*: That everyone was evil at heart.

*Director*: How were you disabused?

*Protégé*: Through people like you.

*Director*: Are there many people like me?

*Protégé*: Alright, only through you. I'm still on alert for evil, but I've known you for a while and I've yet to see it in you.

*Director*: Maybe there's evil but I keep it down.

*Protégé*: Maybe. And if so, that's good.

*Director*: Do you think there's evil in you?

*Protégé*: I know there is.

*Director*: How?

*Protégé*: I've been unnecessarily cruel.

*Director*: Did you enjoy it?

*Protégé*: Honestly? I did.

*Director*: Do you feel guilty about it now?

*Protégé*: No.

*Director*: What were the circumstances?

*Protégé*: A bully tripped and fell one day. His glasses came off. I walked up and crushed them beneath my foot, then walked away.

*Director*: He was a bully toward you?

*Protégé*: He was, yes.

*Director*: What happened after this?

*Protégé*: He showed me new-found respect.

*Director*: Respect for being cruel. Is that what you want to be respected for? Cruelty?

*Protégé*: No. But I'll tell you—it felt good.

*Director*: Then why don't you want that?

*Protégé*: I know it's wrong.

*Director*: How do you know it's wrong? It feels good. Or doesn't it?

*Protégé*: Talking to you, it doesn't feel good.

*Director*: But without me?

*Protégé*: It feels okay.

*Director*: So what will you do? Go to where you feel good or at least okay? Or go to where you feel not so good—with me?

*Protégé*: I'd rather go with you.

*Director*: Why?

*Protégé*: Because I know where each way leads.

*Director*: Where does the glasses-crushing way lead?

*Protégé*: To more cruel acts.

*Director*: What's wrong with that?

*Protégé*: They don't lead anywhere good.

*Director*: They don't lead anywhere good? Or they don't lead anywhere at all?

*Protégé*: They don't lead anywhere at all. It's always the same old thing. Violence.

*Director*: And my way, if it's 'my way' to speak of?

*Protégé*: Philosophy's way? It leads to truth.

*Director*: And truth is what you want above all else?

*Protégé*: Isn't that what you want?

*Director*: I'm not so sure.


## ~ TRUTH, AGAIN


*Director*: There are many truths in the world. Do we need to know them all?

*Protégé*: Do we?

*Director*: I don't know. Maybe. But not if by 'truth' we mean facts.

*Protégé*: Facts not relevant to our lives.

*Director*: Right. So we only care about what's relevant to us?

*Protégé*: That's all that any of us care about.

*Director*: You might be surprised. Don't you have professors in school who care about strange historical facts? While I was waiting for you I saw a syllabus for a class lying on the table. It said that the professor is planning to spend a week on how fabric dyes were set in the eighteenth century. Relevant?

*Protégé*: Not to me. But to the professor? Sure, to furthering his or her career.

*Director*: Is that the key? What helps us get ahead is relevant to us?

*Protégé*: That's what most people think.

*Director*: What's relevant to you? The conjugation of Attic Greek verbs?

*Protégé*: They're relevant to me because I want to read the authors in the original.

*Director*: Why?

*Protégé*: I want to know what they actually said.

*Director*: You don't trust translators?

*Protégé*: Of course I don't.

*Director*: Why not?

*Protégé*: They're not always faithful.

*Director*: To the original? But how can they be?

*Protégé*: What do you mean?

*Director*: We have no precise knowledge of what was actually going on in fifth century Athens. We have many ideas, so to speak, but that's about it.

*Protégé*: But we can say the same about our own era. We have no precise knowledge about what's actually going on in much of twenty-first century America. We have many ideas, but that's about it.

*Director*: Really?

*Protégé*: Really.

*Director*: Then it's a problem.

*Protégé*: That's all you can say?

*Director*: Maybe this is a truth about the world. The hardest era to know is our own.

*Protégé*: But you know other eras. They give you the perspective you need to understand this era.

*Director*: What do you think I know about these other eras?

*Protégé*: Philosophy's role in them.

*Director*: It's true. I've studied a number of eras for this. But I'm persuaded I know very little.

*Protégé*: I'd take very little over nothing any day. I should look to other eras.

*Director*: If you're inclined that way and understand the limits of what you're about, why not? But I wouldn't spend too much time there.

*Protégé*: Where should I spend my time?

*Director*: Looking for friends.


~ DISAPPOINTMENT


*Protégé*: I'm working on that—with you.

*Director*: Yes, but what will you do if you're disappointed?

*Protégé*: What do you mean?

*Director*: What if you win this friend over and he's not all that you thought?

*Protégé*: But I don't think anything of him. I'm just intrigued.

*Director*: That's a good start.

*Protégé*: Is that how it is with everything? It's good to have nothing in mind?

*Director*: Good as a start, yes. Then you can really see.

*Protégé*: And when we do, we have something in mind.

*Director*: Until you start all over again the very next day.

*Protégé*: Then what's the point of having something in mind?

*Director*: Your starting place changes.

*Protégé*: We keep getting closer to the truth?

*Director*: We can say that.

*Protégé*: But it's not true?

*Director*: Truth is elusive. What can I say? Our starting point changes. That's as much as we know.

*Protégé*: But that's so... defeatist!

*Director*: Defeatist? I don't know about that. Aren't we always heading again unto the breach?

*Protégé*: What's the breach?

*Director*: Where the walls of 'truth' have come tumbling down.

*Protégé*: Now I'm confused. We're the ones who knock down these walls?

*Director*: Yes, of course.

*Protégé*: So we can get to the truth within?

*Director*: That's one of the goals of the war.

*Protégé*: The war with the violent.

*Director*: Right.

*Protégé*: What if they win?

*Director*: 'Truth' prevails, possibly forever.

*Protégé*: And if we win?

*Director*: It's once more unto the breach.

*Protégé*: So there is no end to the war, except if we lose. We're always fighting.

*Director*: We certainly are. The violent won't ever let up. Of that I'm sure.


~ BOTH


*Protégé*: Then what can philosophy do? Better still, what's philosophy all about?

*Director*: I thought we already said.

*Protégé*: Yes, but I want to hear it again from a different perspective.

*Director*: Well, that's a good reason. Philosophy is about not being overwhelmed by truth.

*Protégé*: What does that mean? It's about learning to handle as much truth as possible?

*Director*: Yes, but also truth in the dual sense—truth and 'truth'.

*Protégé*: What is 'truth'?

*Director*: That which passes as truth.

*Protégé*: What makes it pass?

*Director*: 'Philosophers'.

*Protégé*: What's a 'philosopher'?

*Director*: Someone who deals in 'truth'.

*Protégé*: Where do we find these 'philosophers'?

*Director*: All over the place. But sometimes in universities.

*Protégé*: Professors of philosophy. But only sometimes?

*Director*: I know professors who profess truthful, weird philosophy. But even they sometimes let 'truth' slip in.

*Protégé*: Do you let them know where you stand on this 'truth'?

*Director*: Oh, I do.

*Protégé*: Look at you grin! Would you ever teach philosophy?

*Director*: Under the right circumstances, sure.

*Protégé*: Circumstances where you could teach the truth?

*Director*: Teach and learn the truth. Philosophy requires openness. It requires the truthful 'I don't know'. That's how we learn. That's how we know. So I would probably have to pay my students as much as they pay me.

*Protégé*: Does taking a salary, with no cost to you, make you a sort of hypocrite?

*Director*: Not if you're not learning anything, no.

*Protégé*: You really should teach.

*Director*: Why?

*Protégé*: Because you're aware of the problems. That makes you valuable, *Director*. Besides, you have principles. Many don't.

*Director*: What principles do I have? And why should I have them? So you can get a handle on me?

*Protégé*: What? Of course not!

*Director*: Tell me. What's a principle you have?

*Protégé*: I.... Why does that matter?

*Director*: I want to see if you practice what you preach.

*Protégé*: I have many principles.

*Director*: Then you should have no trouble naming one.

*Protégé*: It doesn't work like that.

*Director*: How does it work?

*Protégé*: They just have to... come up!


## ~ Coming Up


*Director*: Yes, principles are always popping up.

*Protégé*: You're being sarcastic.

*Director*: Am I? What are principles for?

*Protégé*: Guidance in our lives.

*Director*: I thought that's what reason is for.

*Protégé*: Principles derive from reason.

*Director*: They're like 'reasons' in this way?

*Protégé*: No, not like that.

*Director*: What are they like? How do they differ from reason?

*Protégé*: Principles aren't weird.

*Director*: That's true. In fact, I'd venture that they're the opposite of weird. They're normal. That's what you want, isn't it? You want to be normal.

*Protégé*: I.... Don't you?

*Director*: I want to be what I am. And what I am is a weird philosopher who listens to even weirder reason. Sometimes.

*Protégé*: What about other times?

*Director*: I blend right in with everyone else.

*Protégé*: I'd like to learn that trick.

*Director*: It's really not much of a trick.

*Protégé*: Are you saying you don't always listen to reason?

*Director*: I'll tell you the secret now. Reason, sometimes it doesn't speak.

*Protégé*: What does that mean?

*Director*: Reason is silent at times.

*Protégé*: What do we do then?

*Director*: Most fall back on principles derived from what they know.

*Protégé*: That sounds pretty good. But if reason has the power to shape what we know, then reason has the power, when it speaks once again, to modify our principles. No?

*Director*: Yes.

*Protégé*: How does this work, in practice?

*Director*: Let's take a basic example. I don't lie, on principle. Reason might say there are times when it's okay to lie. Our principle goes from an absolute to one that's qualified. It's as simple as that.

*Protégé*: But it's not that simple for everyone. Why?

*Director*: They don't know how to listen to reason.

*Protégé*: Can they be taught?

*Director*: No.

*Protégé*: No? I find that hard to believe.

*Director*: Do you? You who have always listened to reason?

*Protégé*: But what about the man aged twenty-four who learned to listen to reason?

*Director*: He always had it in him.

*Protégé*: What, circumstances got in the way?

*Director*: It's not quite that simple, but yes.

*Protégé*: So he cleared the way.

*Director*: That's much, don't you think?

*Protégé*: I do. But why can't others listen? Are their circumstances simply too bad?

*Director*: At a certain point we are our circumstances, *Protégé*. Some circumstances are very, very bad.

*Protégé*: And that's it? All the world is as simple as that?

*Director*: The world is both simple and complicated at once. The key is to understand the simple and take it from there.

## ~ THE WORLD

*Protégé*: How do you divide the world?

*Director*: Between those who listen to reason, and those who don't. How do you divide the world?

*Protégé*: Between those who do violence, and those who don't. But I think it's much the same thing.

*Director*: Yes, as we've been saying.

*Protégé*: Are you confident you can tell those who do from those who don't?

*Director*: No, I'm sometimes surprised.

*Protégé*: So what do you do?

*Director*: I proceed with caution.

*Protégé*: How?

*Director*: I ask lots of questions.

*Protégé*: But that annoys people.

*Director*: Is it better to be wrong? And who gets annoyed, what sort of person?

*Protégé*: You have a point. Those who listen to reason are less likely to be annoyed. So how often do you annoy?

*Director*: Often enough that I stay out of trouble—serious trouble, at least.

*Protégé*: I don't ask enough questions.

*Director*: Why not?

*Protégé*: Because I'm shy.

*Director*: Why are you shy?

*Protégé*: Because I'm afraid.

*Director*: Of what?

*Protégé*: The answers to my questions.

*Director*: Those are the most important questions to ask.

*Protégé*: I somehow know that.

*Director*: Then you're not acting on what you know. There's no greater crime.

*Protégé*: Crime?

*Director*: Against yourself. And, by extension, others.

*Protégé*: How in the world do I harm others?

*Director*: Imagine there's a great battle, and our side is all drawn up on the front. If you fail to hold your own, what happens to the rest of us?

*Protégé*: I take the point. But is it really as serious as that?

*Director*: I don't know. I just wanted to get your attention. But it's very serious for you. Nothing could be more serious, in fact.

*Protégé*: I believe it. So what should I ask?

*Director*: Let's start with your friend. The general questions I spoke of, you should ask them of him.

*Protégé*: I can do that. But if the going gets rough, you'll step in?

*Director*: I will step in. Do you know why?

*Protégé*: You want to help me out?

*Director*: It's because I'm afraid.

*Protégé*: Of what?

*Director*: Our side getting overrun.

*Protégé*: I thought you were just making that up.

*Director*: For you, yes. But for me? That's how I look at these things. It's the dominant metaphor in my life.

*Protégé*: I don't have a dominant metaphor.

*Director*: And you may be better than I am for it.

*Protégé*: You really don't mean that.

*Director*: But I do. This metaphor in me may prove to be a crutch.

*Protégé*: Don't you ever let it go?

*Director*: I do. But I keep on coming back. I'm either to be praised as loyal or condemned as a fool.

*Protégé*: Maybe you're something between.


~ BETWEEN


*Director*: You may have discovered what philosophy is.

*Protégé*: Why can't you be serious with me?

*Director*: But I am! Philosophy might be the between.

*Protégé*: Between loyalty and foolishness in what we think?

*Director*: Yes.

*Protégé*: How so?

*Director*: What does loyalty apply to in thought?

*Protégé*: Our principles.

*Director*: And foolishness?

*Protégé*: Throwing those principles away. So how does philosophy walk a line between that?

*Director*: It listens to reason, stays loyal, but makes important exceptions.

*Protégé*: Some see those exceptions as treason.

*Director*: And some see reason as bad. Are we going to live our lives according the judgment of 'some'?

*Protégé*: No, of course not. I actually like what we're saying. But isn't there another name for this, something other than philosophy?

*Director*: Sometimes it's called prudence. Sometimes it's referred to as finding the balance in life. To me, those two are much the same thing.

*Protégé*: I agree. But that's not what philosophy is.

*Director*: What do you mean?

*Protégé*: Philosophy is immoderate in listening to reason. Yes? And don't hedge.

*Director*: What's immoderate about listening to reason? What does immoderate mean? That we do some harm to ourselves by listening to reason? No, *Protégé*. I won't go along with you there.

*Protégé*: But there's no way we can say philosophy is prudence. If you won't admit this, I won't know what to think.

*Director*: What a terrible thing that would be. Okay, I admit it. Philosophy and prudence are very different things.

*Protégé*: What is philosophy?

*Director*: I like your persistence. Philosophy is a sort of constructive criticism.

*Protégé*: I can't believe you're toying with me.

*Director*: But it's true!

*Protégé*: What's the aim of the criticism?

*Director*: To make a better world.

*Protégé*: Now I know you're toying with me!

*Director*: You don't think that's a worthy goal?

*Protégé*: Of course I do! But I don't think it's the goal of philosophy.

*Director*: Then you don't know philosophy well.

*Protégé*: That's why I'm asking you and hoping to get an honest answer.

*Director*: Well, I'll tell you this. I snuck some philosophy into our conversation today. It's up to you to figure out where.

*Protégé*: There's only been some?

*Director*: What do you expect? A full dose of my teaching for free?

*Protégé*: Don't smirk at me like that.

*Director*: I think you can't see what philosophy is because it's right under your nose.

*Protégé*: Help me look under my nose.

*Director*: Please believe me. I'm doing all I can. But I'm afraid.

*Protégé*: Of what?

*Director*: If I get too close you might sneeze.


~ Close


*Protégé*: Because I'm allergic to you?

*Director*: Because you're human.

*Protégé*: How close can human beings get?

*Director*: I've found that it's prudent to keep a little distance.

*Protégé*: How little is a little?

*Director*: I'd go no more than how I'm going with you today.

*Protégé*: Have you really been that open with me?

*Director*: Have you with me?

*Protégé*: I take your point. Somehow I find this sad.

*Director*: Sad that we preserve healthy boundaries?

*Protégé*: That 'healthy boundaries' stuff comes from therapists.

*Director*: Sometimes they get it right. But why do you feel sad?

*Protégé*: Because I want more. Oh, not specifically from you. In general, *Director*.

*Director*: You wish we of this world could be closer than we are.

*Protégé*: I do.

*Director*: You who have so few friends.

*Protégé*: I don't have any friends, to tell you the truth.

*Director*: Maybe that's the problem. Let's see what you say after a couple of months of Greek verbs.

*Protégé*: You might be right. I'll suspend my judgment here.

*Director*: I'm impressed. That's no small feat for something as urgent as this.

*Protégé*: How do you know it's urgent?

*Director*: Don't you know what philosophers pride themselves on most? They always know what's urgent.

*Protégé*: How do they know?

*Director*: They find a way to get in close. And then they can feel, positively feel the pressure there.

*Protégé*: Pressure causes urgency?

*Director*: What else would?

*Protégé*: And you think I'm under pressure to find a friend.

*Director*: Yes. I would be that friend, but you need someone more your age.

*Protégé*: Someone who's not a philosopher?

*Director*: That's not a requirement, no. Though it's hard for philosophers to be friends with philosophers. They can be on friendly terms, certainly. Sometimes not so friendly, too. But two philosophers together will all but fall into a trance, listening as they do to reason.

*Protégé*: A trance doesn't sound so bad right now.

*Director*: That's because you've yet to discover the joys of friendship.

*Protégé*: I feel pretty good right here with you.

*Director*: So do I. With you, I mean.

*Protégé*: There is no violence here.

*Director*: None that I'm aware of, no.

*Protégé*: So why can't we be friends?

*Director*: We are friends. But know this—I refuse to be your crutch.

*Protégé*: Ouch!

*Director*: I'm sorry, but it's true. I want you, more than you know, to stand on your own two feet.

~ STANDING

*Protégé*: How do I do that?

*Director*: You start by making friends.

*Protégé*: So you'll be my training wheels here.

*Director*: Yes, with your potential friend. But then I'm going away.

*Protégé*: For good?

*Director*: No, not for good. But your friends are up to you.

*Protégé*: And I need to understand them for what they are.

*Director*: Of course.

*Protégé*: If I misunderstand, I do violence to them.

*Director*: And yourself. But try to remember, through thick and thin—friends either listen to reason or not. That's all you need to know.

*Protégé*: Is it really that simple?

*Director*: Yes, and it's very hard to remember when in their midst. But in another sense it's complex. Some people listen to reason here; some people listen to reason there.

*Protégé*: It's not black and white. There are shades of gray.

*Director*: Just so. And the gray can overwhelm, can knock you off your feet.

*Protégé*: So we don't judge people in absolutes.

*Director*: Not unless they absolutely do or don't listen to reason.

*Protégé*: Are there such people?

*Director*: I don't know. Maybe for a time, while under a passion.

*Protégé*: I can see how passions can cause you to fail to listen. But how can a passion make you hear?

*Director*: You really don't know? There is such a thing as a passion for reason. And it drives some people wild.

*Protégé*: But you're suggesting that this can't be good. I thought listening to reason is always good.

*Director*: Listening requires no passion. Listening with a passion means we're failing to hear.

*Protégé*: What are those like who listen but fail to hear?

*Director*: They're maniacs. They run around proclaiming reason to anyone with ears. But those with ears don't need to hear reason from them. They hear it well enough on their own.

*Protégé*: So these maniacs are uncouth.

*Director*: Yes.

*Protégé*: What's the harm?

*Director*: Think of it this way. A doctor thinks you may have cancer, and wants to break it to you gently, and explain that you might not have it—it's not yet clear. The uncouth run into the room shouting, 'Cancer! Cancer!' And they laugh.

*Protégé*: I think that sums it up. But how did they know to come into the room?

*Director*: They heard tell of cancer at reason's well.

*Protégé*: What's their passion?

*Director*: I'm not sure. Maybe they love to be the bearer of news?

*Protégé*: Yes, some people do have a passion for that. But maybe their passion is that they're new to reason and they're overwhelmed with excitement.

*Director*: That happens, yes. Reason can be exciting.

*Protégé*: But only for a while.

*Director*: Why only for a while?

*Protégé*: Because we need to find a way to share it, and we often can't. Then the excitement dies down.

*Director*: So we look for more reason and get excited again.

*Protégé*: But who do we share it with?

*Director*: We share it quietly with those who have ears to hear.


~ QUIETLY


*Protégé*: Why quietly?

*Director*: Because we'd rather not be uncouth.

*Protégé*: No, seriously. Why quietly?

*Director*: Don't you remember? Reason always speaks in a quiet and gentle voice. To speak reason quietly is in keeping with the thing.

*Protégé*: And we should always be in keeping with the thing?

*Director*: Think of pets.

*Protégé*: Pets?

*Director*: Do you think if you have a cat it's best to be in keeping with feline or canine things?

*Protégé*: Feline, of course. Is that how it always is? As simple as that?

*Director*: Always, as far as I know. Though the example has its limits. There are other things where the appropriate in-keeping isn't so clear.

*Protégé*: How can we learn what's appropriate?

*Director*: There's only one way. We get to know the things.

*Protégé*: What if we're dealing with violent things?

*Director*: We give those things what they deserve.

*Protégé*: And if these things are somehow obscured from view?

*Director*: We flush them out by speaking reason with pride.

*Protégé*: They'll almost certainly react to that.

*Director*: Yes.

*Protégé*: And if they don't?

*Director*: It's very likely they're dead.

*Protégé*: We should always speak reason with pride.

*Director*: Why should we?

*Protégé*: Because we're proud of what we are.

*Director*: And what are we?

*Protégé*: Good.

*Director*: Reason isn't simply good.

*Protégé*: What is it?

*Director*: Indifferent to pride.

*Protégé*: I don't know what that means.

*Director*: It means reason... just is.

*Protégé*: That's the best you can do?

*Director*: What can I say?

*Protégé*: Oh, it's alright. I think I understand.

*Director*: Do you? That's more than I do.

*Protégé*: You're teasing.

*Director*: Sometimes I say things that make sense to others that I don't understand.

*Protégé*: You don't understand the others, or you don't understand the things you said?

*Director*. If I don't understand what I've said, how can I understand those who do?

*Protégé*: Okay, that's fair. And maybe that's why you speak quietly.

*Director*: Why?

*Protégé*: Because you don't understand what you're saying. You're sort of like a prophet that way. What? What's wrong?

*Director*: I'm no prophet.

*Protégé*: I said you're sort of like one! I didn't mean that you're actually a prophet.

*Director*: You'd better explain.

*Protégé*: Look at you get all upset! I didn't think it was possible. But okay, here's what I think. Prophets are mouthpieces for a god. You, sometimes, in a certain way, are the mouthpiece of reason. Are you upset with me now?

*Director*: No, and I think you make a good point. I'm sorry I got tense. I'm human, you know.

*Protégé*: Now I do. And thank you for trusting me enough to show that to me.

 

~ TRUST

 

*Director*: Why didn't you think it was possible for me to get upset?

*Protégé*: I've never seen you that way.

*Director*: What do you think makes me upset?

*Protégé*: Careless unreason.

*Director*: You impress me again. Can you say more?

*Protégé*: I thoughtlessly compared you to something you're emphatically not.

*Director*: The mouthpiece of a god.

*Protégé*: Yes. And you know I'm not thoughtless. That, more than my comparison, upset you. You don't like to see a thoughtful friend grow thoughtless.

*Director*: You've impressed me further. What you say is true. But you said something about trust. Please say more.

*Protégé*: If you didn't trust me, you would have buried your feelings—or maybe you wouldn't have felt them at all. Either way, to show what you showed, that can only be done among intimates.

*Director*: You and I are close.

*Protégé*: And now I understand why you say we need some distance. It's to prevent misunderstandings like this, or at least to render them less... damaging.

*Director*: What is damaged?

*Protégé*: Our friendship?

*Director*: No. That's as strong as ever.

*Protégé*: Nothing is damaged?

*Director*: There has been no damage done. In fact, good has been done.

*Protégé*: The good of understanding?

*Director*: Yes. But understanding sometimes comes with pain.

*Protégé*: I know that all too well.

*Director*: Do you think understanding can come without pain?

*Protégé*: Yes.

*Director*: How?

*Protégé*: Something just clicks inside. It's as if something cracks our safe, knows the combination.

*Director*: You've described it in exactly the opposite way most people would.

*Protégé*: Most people would say it's we who crack the safe—active not passive.

*Director*: Yes. But somehow your way makes sense. Do you know what this means?

*Protégé*: I don't. Tell me.

*Director*: I'm utterly at sea.

*Protégé*: First you get cross, and now you're lost? What have I done!

*Director*: I don't know, *Protégé*. But keep on doing it!

*Protégé*: You like to be cross and lost?

*Director*: Of course not. But these things are signs I'm on my way to learning something new.

*Protégé*: If only you can stay composed and find your way.

*Director*: Yes. And here's the thing. I don't expect help from you.

*Protégé*: Ah.

*Director*: Ah what?

*Protégé*: You're trying to be an example to me. And it makes me think you might not be lost at all!

*Director*: Oh, I'm lost. Violence—my violence—has that effect on me. Besides, if I were faking—what kind of example would I be?

*Protégé*: A bad one.

*Director*: Yes. I mean what I say, my friend. And I show as much as I can.


~ SHOW


*Protégé*: Why can't we show everything?

*Director*: Because we all have some degree of violence within. For instance, when I'm angry, I think violent thoughts. Should I share those thoughts?

*Protégé*: No, I take your point. But something about that bothers me.

*Director*: What?

*Protégé*: Reason should always be shared, yes?

*Director*: When possible, yes.

*Protégé*: Well, if there is thought that shouldn't be shared, that means thought and reason aren't the same thing.

*Director*: They're not. Thinking is different than reason. Reason is weird; thinking is not.

*Protégé*: I'm not sure I understand why that is, why thinking can't be weird. I mean, we can think weird things, can't we?

*Director*: You have a point. And I'm not going to make a stand on the distinction between reason and thought. I'm just telling you how it seems to me.

*Protégé*: I think we should share weird thoughts with friends.

*Director*: Well, since you mention it, I'll tell you this. When I wrestle with my anger, I sometimes come to think weird thoughts that I want to share with friends.

*Protégé*: That makes the wrestling worthwhile.

*Director*: Yes. I try to use my anger to our advantage. But why do you think the wrestling is good? Can you say?

*Protégé*: It's simple. Reason is weird. Your weird thoughts, if not identical to reason, are at least akin. Reason is good. Weird thoughts are good, in their kinship to reason. It's good to share good things with friends. How's that?

*Director*: Not bad. But we have to ask—what is good? In other words, what makes something good?

*Protégé*: Why do we have to ask that? We know reason is good. Or are you going to tell me reason is somehow beyond good?

*Director*: I was going to, but now I'm not so sure.

*Protégé*: You're not sure if you're going to tell me that?

*Director*: Right. Because now I don't know if it's true.

*Protégé*: You're too easy to steer and persuade.

*Director*: That's only because I'm with you. And do you know what this means?

*Protégé*: That I'm a philosopher?

*Director*: No, though you may be. I was thinking it means we're on the right path. Both of us are open to persuasion right now. Reason has opened us up.

*Protégé*: Then let's talk some more about bad thoughts.

*Director*: Let's

*Protégé*: I think if we think bad thoughts, thinking still is good.

*Director*: I'm inclined that way, too. But I have to come back to the question. What does it mean to be good?

*Protégé*: For lack of a better definition, I'll say good is something that does us well.

*Director*: Does us well?

*Protégé*: What can I say?

*Director*: Okay. Since I have nothing better to contribute, let's go with that. So thinking bad thoughts does us well?

*Protégé*: I'll answer by saying this. Those who never think bad thoughts cannot do themselves well.

*Director*: Why not?

*Protégé*: Because they're living in a dream.

*Director*: What's wrong with dreams?

*Protégé*: They're not true!

*Director*: What's so good about true?

*Protégé*: You ask that question because you care about truth.

*Director*: Truth is truth without any care from me.

*Protégé*: But truth isn't generally known.

*Director*: What truth do you want to know?

*Protégé*: I want you to speak about yourself.

*Director*: You want me to show you who I am?

*Protégé*: Yes.

*Director*: You can figure that out yourself—maybe better than I can say.

*Protégé*: Oh, don't say that.

*Director*: Why not?

*Protégé*: Because I need to believe it's possible for me to show myself who I am.

*Director*: Who are you?

*Protégé*: A philosopher.

*Director*: Sure. But what does that mean?

*Protégé*: You're a philosopher. Why should you ask?

*Director*: Because 'philosopher' is just a word. How do I know what it means to you? What if it means something very different to me?

*Protégé*: That's what we need to find out.

*Director*: How will we do it? By tossing words and meanings about?

*Protégé*: You tell me.

*Director*: I think we'll see when we meet with your friend. If you're a philosopher, we'll know.

*Protégé*: We'll know? How will I know?

*Director*: If you're a philosopher, you will know.


~ KNOWING, AGAIN


*Protégé*: That's not a very satisfying answer, you know.

*Director*: Do you agree we're not always satisfied with everything someone says?

*Protégé*: Of course.

*Director*: Well, a philosopher asks about the unsatisfying things. Do you ask?

*Protégé*: I just asked you!

*Director*: Yes, but do you ask others?

*Protégé*: I usually just keep quiet. Does that mean I'm not a philosopher?

*Director*: It means you're not one yet, at least.

*Protégé*: But there are so many unsatisfying things! Do I ask about them all?

*Director*: No. You have to choose your battles. Is that what you do?

*Protégé*: I... don't really battle.

*Director*: Definitely not a philosopher yet.

*Protégé*: How will I know when to fight?

*Director*: When you know there's a chance of winning.

*Protégé*: How will I know?

*Director*: There will be signs.

*Protégé*: What sort of signs?

*Director*: You'll have to say something weird and see how the person reacts.

*Protégé*: What sort of reaction am I looking for?

*Director*: If they're intrigued, you have a chance. Any other reaction is bad.

*Protégé*: Even if they completely agree with the weird thing I said?

*Director*: That's a sign you failed to say something weird.

*Protégé*: I see. But what if the weirdness drives them away?

*Director*: Do you really want friends who can't handle the weird?

*Protégé*: No, because that means they can't handle reason. I want friends who can.

*Director*: Yes, but sometimes life gets in the way of the friendship,

*Protégé*: Life gets in the way. I never liked that expression. What does it mean here?

*Director*: You'll both have to fight—and fight, for the most part, on your own.

*Protégé*: Why not fight together?

*Director*: Because, for one, that cuts the number of battles you can fight in half. There's an urgent need for fighters, fighters who know how to fight.

*Protégé*: So you'll train me and then turn me loose to fight on my own?

*Director*: Yes.

*Protégé*: And this applies to all true friends?

*Director*: All who listen to gentle, sweet reason—yes. We fight on our own. Oh, but that doesn't mean we can't get together when there's a lull in the battle.

*Protégé*: Good. I was wondering about that.

*Director*: And think how good it will be to get together then.

*Protégé*: But, *Director*, is there ever a lull? Violence is everywhere. It happens all the time.

*Director*: Our time for rest is short. But we have it. And we need to use it to help shore each other up.

*Protégé*: We strengthen our resolve.

*Director*: Yes.

*Protégé*: We help heal each other's wounds.

*Director*: Of course.

*Protégé*: We leave each other energized for another fight.

*Director*: We certainly do.

*Protégé*: But what does all of this really mean? Today you and I are together; tomorrow you go back to work.

*Director*: And that's it. Nothing too crazy here. My battle is mostly at work.

*Protégé*: Where is my battle?

*Director*: Don't you know? Your battle is here.

*Protégé*: With you?

*Director*: If you find violent unreason in me? Yes. But I was thinking about your school. There's plenty of violence there. So try and pull some friends out of the melee and give them a dose of the weird.


## ~ SOURCES


*Protégé*: What are the biggest sources of violence here at school?

*Director*: I think there are two. One, the professors; two, the students.

*Protégé*: What comes from the students?

*Director*: Opinions they bring from home.

*Protégé*: That's it?

*Director*: These opinions are often ossified into bone. Good luck trying to work with them. Reason stands no chance. And those who have no flexibility often become enemies of those who do. They attack. Sound familiar?

*Protégé*: Yes. What about the professors?

*Director*: They sometimes show some flexibility. Some even show a good amount. But there are certain lines they will not cross. Come near those lines and they will attack.

*Protégé*: And when they attack, we're not talking about yelling and screaming, are we?

*Director*: No, we're not. Most often the professors speak in a sweet and gentle tone, trying to show they're akin to reason. And they may be. But not all kin are good.

*Protégé*: You don't have to tell me. But why won't they cross those lines?

*Director*: I'm not sure. Maybe life would seem weird if they did and they're afraid of that? Or maybe those lines are the supports on which they've built their lives? Maybe both.

*Protégé*: Those could be the reasons for the students' attacks, too.

*Director*: A good observation. Maybe violent unreason is always the same.

*Protégé*: That would make those who attack reason all the same. They aren't true individuals. They're some kind of... of....

*Director*: Collective of the dead.

*Protégé*: Yes! We only live to the extent we listen to reason. Reason is the source of life.

*Director*: I can go along with that. But those who listen to reason, people like us—they are individuated?

*Protégé*: They are.

*Director*: How?

*Protégé*: Even if reason is always the same, the facts reasoned upon differ. We all have different facts in our lives. When we reason on them, we individuate ourselves.

*Director*: We're different because we all do the same thing?

*Protégé*: Exactly.

*Director*: Hmm.

*Protégé*: What is it?

*Director*: It feels like a stretch. Why not say we're all the same in what counts? Reason. Or are you so hung up on individualism that you'd rather not?

*Protégé*: I don't want to be hung up on any -ism.

*Director*: Then don't be hung up here.

*Protégé*: Tell me something, *Director*. Can there be violence that isn't violence against reason?

*Director*: An interesting question. I suppose it's possible. I mean, the violent do violence to the violent all the time.

*Protégé*: Why?

*Director*: They fight over differing false opinions.

*Protégé*: That makes sense. But I don't see why they bother. It just seems pointless. Why hold on the way they do?

*Director*: I think it's because they're cowards. It takes courage to let go of an opinion and test it in a wash of truth.

*Protégé*: It's funny, because they think we're cowards for never doing violence to anything.

*Director*: I'd do violence to them if they did violence to my friends or me.

*Protégé*: I don't doubt it. But is this because of your metaphor, the battlefront?

*Director*: I sometimes wonder. Which came first? Violence in my disposition? Or a metaphor that encourages violence in me?

*Protégé*: Does it matter?

*Director*: I thought you might tell me.


~ Metaphors


*Protégé*: Here's the thing. Reason doesn't speak in metaphors.

*Director*: True. We use metaphors to help us interpret reason.

*Protégé*: I think metaphors do violence, however little, to reason.

*Director*: Do you think we can get by without doing a touch of violence to reason?

*Protégé*: Can we live a life of pure reason? I think it's impossible. We're human, after all.

*Director*: So we need some degree of violence?

*Protégé*: Yes, but innocent violence, like kittens at play.

*Director*: I like what you're saying. Maybe that's what we should do with the violent—play with them.

*Protégé*: That will drive them crazy!

*Director*: And do you know what will drive them crazier?

*Protégé*: Tell me.

*Director*: While we play we slip in the weird.

*Protégé*: Ha! They'll hate that! But what we should really do is speak the weird in a very loud voice so everyone around us can hear!

*Director*: Do you really want everyone to know you're in touch with the weird? That might be a lot to take on at once.

*Protégé*: You have a point. I'll take things a step at a time.

*Director*: Good. But what's your metaphor, the metaphor as the backdrop to your life?

*Protégé*: You're going to think I'm foolish.

*Director*: Maybe. Tell me.

*Protégé*: I've already suggested it. Playful kittens.

*Director*: I envision a terrible global battlefield. You envision... kittens. The funny thing is, I think we're equally right.

*Protégé*: You really think so?

*Director*: I do. But I want to see how this metaphor serves you, serves the cause.

*Protégé*: I hope to show you. But I noticed that you're suggesting I'm at one with the cause.

*Director*: I've come to think you are.

*Protégé*: You weren't sure?

*Director*: I had my doubts. And I think you have a long way to go. But so do I.

*Protégé*: Tell me something about the violent. Do you ever have doubts about them?

*Director*: About whether they're violent and nothing more? I do.

*Protégé*: What do you do when you do?

*Director*: I put them to the test.

*Protégé*: You say something weird?

*Director*: I do. But I wrap it in a metaphor to disguise what I'm doing.

*Protégé*: What kind of a metaphor?

*Director*: One I think won't suit reason quite well.

*Protégé*: What do you look for then?

*Director*: If they say it's a comfortable fit, and they notice nothing strange, I'm dealing with someone who is blind, deaf, or dumb.

*Protégé*: Blind because they can't see it doesn't really fit? Deaf because they don't hear reason's quiet voice? Dumb because even if they do notice something isn't right, they can't speak the words to say what it is?

*Director*: Yes.

*Protégé*: But I feel bad for the dumb. Can't we teach them how to say what they feel?

*Director*: Remember, we're talking about the violent. What do you think they feel?

*Protégé*: Rage?

*Director*: That could very well be. Do we want to teach them how to give voice to that rage?

*Protégé*: I think we do, Director.

*Director*: Why?

*Protégé*: Because it's better to let rage out in words than to bottle it up until it explodes.

*Director*: I see there's a therapist in you.

*Protégé*: You know, I've considered majoring in that, therapy. Do you really think I'd make a good therapist?

*Director*: I think you'd make an excellent therapist. If I were you, I'd look into it more.

### ~ THERAPY

*Protégé*: Thank you. I will definitely look into it further. But now there's something I want to know. We've touched on therapy for the violent dumb. What about therapy for the gentle?

*Director*: The first thing I think you have to do is reinforce with them that listening to reason is good.

*Protégé*: Why that?

*Director*: Because of violent attacks, some of the reasonable come to believe that reason is bad, the source of their trouble. You have to help them see this isn't so.

*Protégé*: How do I do that?

*Director*: By offering praise.

*Protégé*: It's that simple?

*Director*: To someone in the desert something to drink is all. Offer cool water, friend.

*Protégé*: I'll lead them to an oasis.

*Director*: Yes, that's an excellent thing to do. Let your therapy sessions be the oasis.

*Protégé*: And over time I'll teach them that sweet reason is the oasis.

*Director*: Yes. And you can tell them to pitch their tents there. No need to wander in the desert any more.

*Protégé*: I think I can do some good.

*Director*: I know you can do some good—much good, in fact.

*Protégé*: Thank you.

*Director*: For what?

*Protégé*: Helping me find my way.

*Director*: You found it on your own. I just put a name to the thing I saw. Therapy. But you were already thinking that long before today. No?

*Protégé*: It's true.

*Director*: Why do you think you were attracted here, to therapy?

*Protégé*: Because I have strong empathy.

*Director*: Do you empathize with me?

*Protégé*: I empathize with how you must feel about your global fight.

*Director*: And how must I feel?

*Protégé*: Outnumbered and all but overwhelmed. Is that how you feel?

*Director*: Are you conducting therapy on me?

*Protégé*: I can, if you want.

*Director*: Why not? Yes, you've guessed how I feel—at times.

*Protégé*: Those times when you feel this way, what do you do?

*Director*: I fall back and try to regroup.

*Protégé*: Regroup? You fight this fight with others?

*Director*: I do. I have friends who share this metaphor with me. But, even so, we fight alone.

*Protégé*: And what do you do? Plan your attacks?

*Director*: Yes, we coordinate our solo efforts for maximum effect.

*Protégé*: That sounds good.

*Director*: It is. What therapy do I need?

*Protégé*: Maybe none. But I'll invite you to the oasis, nonetheless.

*Director*: There's war in the desert, you know.

*Protégé*: I know. Will you come to my oasis?

*Director*: I will.

*Protégé*: You'd really have me as your therapist?

*Director*: Of course! I always talk to those who truly want to talk to me.

*Protégé*: Now you're making it sound like you'll be a therapist to me!

*Director*: And I will. Don't you know? The very best therapy goes both ways.


## ~ ONE WAY

*Protégé*: I think many therapists treat therapy as a one-way street.

*Director*: And that's too bad. They don't allow themselves to learn. Good therapists do. But there's something more unfortunate here.

*Protégé*: What?

*Director*: One-way therapists often do violence to their patients.

*Protégé*: How?

*Director*: They judge.

*Protégé*: But that's the one thing therapists are taught—not to judge.

*Director*: The only way not to judge is to learn. Not all therapists learn. And that makes therapists bad.

*Protégé*: Because when we judge we can't hear soft reason.

*Director*: Exactly. And I'm not saying we never need to judge. I judge people as violent beyond repair all the time. But the therapist's world should be an oasis, as you've said.

*Protégé*: What if I have a patient, a client, who shows all the signs of violence beyond repair? Do I show them the oasis?

*Director*: To them it will seem a mirage. No, you let them blow off steam, and that's about it.

*Protégé*: If I get to the point where I can afford to choose my clients, I will only choose those who need the oasis.

*Director*: Maybe keep one or two of the violent about.

*Protégé*: For what?

*Director*: As reminders of what's out there.

*Protégé*: How could I ever forget?

*Director*: For some of us it's easy to forget. It's a sort of defense. Does that make sense to you?

*Protégé*: I think it does.

*Director*: Well, we need reminders, unpleasant as they are.

*Protégé*: Philosophy has to return to the cave.

*Director*: What did you say?

*Protégé*: It's from Plato's Republic. We philosophers travel up to the light. But then we have to return to the dark cave below.

*Director*: No, that's foolishness. Stay in the light. But take a peek at the cave every so often to see what's going on. Make sure they're not planning some assault on the light.

*Protégé*: Okay. I will. Do you ever lead raids into the darkness of the cave?

*Director*: Not often. But I do keep watch on the entrance. If someone like you comes out, I hasten to lend support until your eyes have adjusted to the light. But if a violent soul comes out? I lie in wait.

*Protégé*: What do you do?

*Director*: I kill them.

*Protégé*: What!

*Director*: Just kidding. I turn them around and send them back into the cave.

*Protégé*: They don't resist?

*Director*: I hardly have to lift a finger. The light drives them right back in.

*Protégé*: Then why do you stand watch if the light does all the work?

*Director*: Because, Protégé, I'm looking for people like you. And, besides, if enough come out at once, in a great assault, they might make it far enough into the sunshine to do some serious harm.

*Protégé*: To people like you and me.

*Director*: Correct.

*Protégé*: What do we do if there's such an assault?

*Director*: Keep retreating and stringing them along so that the light can eventually do its work.

*Protégé*: And turn them to dust?

*Director*: That would be nice. But usually they become disheartened and head back to the cave. So, no matter what, don't do this.

*Protégé*: What?

*Director*: Give them succor.

*Protégé*: How would I do that?

*Director*: By giving them metaphorical shade.

*Protégé*: Encouragement?

*Director*: Yes. No giving comfort to the enemy. Let them try for their comfort back in the cave.


### ~ Bombs


*Protégé*: I had a terrible thought.

*Director*: Please share it.

*Protégé*: What if we lobbed a bomb into the cave? Couldn't we take out all the violent at once?

*Director*: I suppose we could. But there's a problem.

*Protégé*: What problem?

*Director*: Some of those in the cave might belong to the light.

*Protégé*: Oh, of course. What was I thinking? That is a problem.

*Director*: We have to be targeted in our attacks.

*Protégé*: I agree. But maybe the bomb we toss doesn't kill them all at once.

*Director*: What does it do?

*Protégé*: It flushes everyone out of the cave.

*Director*: And that's a good thing?

*Protégé*: It's good because we can see who is beyond all hope and who has a chance. We grab those with a chance and pull them aside before everyone else goes back in once the dust has settled.

*Director*: I like what you're saying. And then we send those with a chance to therapy with you. But some will resist, no?

*Protégé*: Of course. People often resist therapy—many times those who stand to gain the most.

*Director*: So we have to let them go back if they want to go back.

*Protégé*: Yes, but we patiently await their return.

*Director*: And if they never come back?

*Protégé*: It's very sad.

*Director*: What if a person goes back to the cave, tells those there exactly where we are, and helps plan the next assault? That could happen, couldn't it?

*Protégé*: Yes, it could. And it would be terrible in its effect.

*Director*: What can we do?

*Protégé*: Keep moving around. Don't give them set targets to hit.

*Director*: To be sure, this is a metaphor?

*Protégé*: Yes, of course.

*Director*: What does it mean to metaphorically move around?

*Protégé*: We change what we say.

*Director*: We contradict ourselves?

*Protégé*: No, we just don't always say the same things.

*Director*: But won't that confuse those we're trying to persuade? Don't we have to gently repeat ourselves over and over again until it sinks in?

*Protégé*: Sure, but let's suppose we're trying to teach someone about a sphere. One day we use apples; another day we use oranges. One day we use marbles; another day we use a basketball. One day we use the Earth; another day we use the Moon. All of this is to get the point across without being stuck on the same thing.

*Director*: So examples, metaphors will change. But not the basic point.

*Protégé*: Never the basic point.

*Director*: And while there is a fixed target—reason—the violent enemy can never know where that is.

*Protégé*: If they knew, they'd be on our side.

*Director*: You're sure about that? Can't there be traitors to reason? Those who know but rebel?

*Protégé*: But why rebel against reason?

*Director*: Because the force of false opinion is all too strong.

*Protégé*: But if a traitor knows where to plant a bomb, right at reason's source....

*Director*: Yes, that might be the end—or so it sometimes seems to me.


## ~ THREATS


*Protégé*: Sometimes? You mean it's not really a threat?

*Director*: I persuade myself it isn't, but stand close watch nonetheless.

*Protégé*: Why wouldn't it be a threat?

*Director*: It's like you were saying. If you know enough to know where reason Is, you are, by definition, not someone who would ever do reason harm

*Protégé*: What if our definition is wrong?

*Director*: I don't think it is.

*Protégé*: To know reason is to love it?

*Director*: Something like that, yes. The real danger, I think, comes from those just taking up with reason. False opinion carries them away and they attack the part they think they know.

*Protégé*: That's still a problem.

*Director*: It is, because the part they think they know might be home to those who are carefully making their way to full reason.

*Protégé*: Students.

*Director*: Yes, students of reason.

*Protégé*: But we're all students in a way. So this is a threat to us all.

*Director*: I'm afraid there's nothing to be done. We can't force traitors to stay in the light. And if they come to us with a desire to learn, we teach, even though we doubt. Life is dangerous, friend. We have to take risks.

*Protégé*: If I spend time helping someone come toward reason, and someone does violence to them, a violence that drives them cowering away—I'd want revenge.

*Director*: No more kittens at play?

*Protégé*: I'm serious, *Director*.

*Director*: And so am I. Do you want the battlefront metaphor now?

*Protégé*: Maybe not that, but something along those lines.

*Director*: Well, brood on it a while and see what comes to mind.

*Protégé*: Brood? Is that a reasonable thing to do?

*Director*: Is revenge a reasonable thing?

*Protégé*: If it prevents further harm to others? I think it can be, yes.

*Director*: Then brood a while on revenge, and see what you think. But tell me now. What sort of revenge do you have in mind?

*Protégé*: Physical revenge—and I don't mean the physicality of the brain.

*Director*: But our words can strike the brain with terrible force. We just have to find the right words.

*Protégé*: Terrible force sounds good.

*Director*: Yes, but it's best for this strike to be gentle.

*Protégé*: Why?

*Director*: Because if the strike is violent, the ear has time to warn the brain. But if the strike is gentle, it passes unnoticed through the ear until it hits its inner target with the desired terrible force.

*Protégé*: I like that.

*Director*: So stay gentle, even in revenge.

*Protégé*: I will.


## ~ HATRED


*Protégé*: I think that gentleness might make them hate us all the more.

*Director*: Why?

*Protégé*: Because it shows such control, a control they don't have.

*Director*: Those who do violence are always out of control?

*Protégé*: In varying degrees, yes. And it makes them ugly—and they know it.

*Director*: They think we're beautiful?

*Protégé*: They know it in their bones. And they hate us for it. They want to mar our beauty however they can.

*Director*: They want to push us until we lose control.

*Protégé*: Exactly. That's a victory for them.

*Director*: Victory in making us like them. But is that how it goes for all of us?

*Protégé*: What do you mean?

*Director*: Do we all want to make others in our own image? The ugly want us to be ugly like them. And we, we want the ugly to be beautiful like us.

*Protégé*: Yes, but there's a difference.

*Director*: What difference?

*Protégé*: Everyone has the potential to be ugly. But not everyone has the potential to be beautiful.

*Director*: Reason is not available to all?

*Protégé*: Isn't that what you think?

*Director*: Yes. But I'm not sure it doesn't go the other way, too.

*Protégé*: Not all of us can be ugly?

*Director*: Some of us can't help but be beautiful, my friend.

*Protégé*: That's... liberating!

*Director*: I agree. Do you think it's true?

*Protégé*: I want to think about it, look around, and see.

*Director*: That sounds like a very good plan. I'll do the same. And then let's compare notes.

*Protégé*: Agreed. But if it's true, that's even more reason to be hated by the violent at heart. I think we have to take precautions.

*Director*: What sort of precautions?

*Protégé*: We have to disguise ourselves.

*Director*: So we won't be attacked?

*Protégé*: Yes. We reveal our true beauty only to the gentle, to those who appreciate the beauty for what it is.

*Director*: Then I wonder what you think of this. Suppose that two people approach. One a known hater of beauty; another his kin who shows signs of appreciation of beauty. What do we do?

*Protégé*: Try to get the kin alone.

*Director*: But let's say we can't, and this is our only opportunity to talk to them. What do we do?

*Protégé*: We start a conversation then slip in something weird.

*Director*: The violent one will attack us for this.

*Protégé*: Yes. But we have to be brave. We have to show the kin that we so love reason that we're willing to be attacked. We press the point.

*Director*: Why?

*Protégé*: Because we want to show the kin that you can resist, that it's possible. And it's not the end of the world.

*Director*: Maybe not for us, but for the kin? Resistance to violence might be the end of the world as they know it.

*Protégé*: But not the end of the world as they don't yet know it.

*Director*: That's true. That world is just beginning.

*Protégé*: And we must show them this.

## ~ Beginnings

*Director*: The core of reason, what do you think it's about?

*Protégé*: Beginnings. Eternal beginnings.

*Director*: Why that?

*Protégé*: Because reason always starts anew. That's why we can have endless conversations. Each time, even if it's about the same old things, it's entirely new.

*Director*: One can tell you're young.

*Protégé*: What's that supposed to mean?

*Director*: Reason, in its core, is also about endings. Eternal endings.

*Protégé*: Why that?

*Director*: Because reason always points to an end.

*Protégé*: To point to an end is different than to end.

*Director*: True. Just as to point to beginnings is different than to begin.

*Protégé*: What's your point? That reason doesn't go anywhere?

*Director*: Reason is, in a sense, immobile. Reason just is. More often than not what we take away from reason is what we brought with us, just more clearly known.

*Protégé*: So you're saying I bring beginnings to reason?

*Director*: Yes.

*Protégé*: And you bring endings?

*Director*: I bring endings. When you age in years you tend to do that more. But I also bring beginnings.

*Protégé*: Is it a fifty-fifty split? Half beginnings, half endings?

*Director*: No, it's ninety-some beginnings and a handful of endings. I'm trying to narrow the endings down to just a very few.

*Protégé*: You're talking about your ending.

*Director*: That's the ending that concerns me, yes.

*Protégé*: But who are the beginnings for?

*Director*: You're going to think I'm selfish. They're for me.

*Protégé*: What are you going to do with ninety-or-so beginnings?

*Director*: Use them as wisely as I can, so that when I come to my end, I can account for and own up to them all.

*Protégé*: You think we should all do that?

*Director*: Yes, I do.

*Protégé*: That puts a lot of pressure on us.

*Director*: Don't think about pressure. Think about the playful kittens. They're a sort of beginning.

*Protégé*: I suppose that's true. But I feel foolish that I need them so.

*Director*: Why? There's real beauty in kittens at play. Never feel foolish about a beautiful thing. To do so is foolish.

*Protégé*: Alright. But what if I only have one beginning and take it all the way to the end?

*Director*: You'd be a sort of hero to me.

*Protégé*: Be serious.

*Director*: I am. I, who have had many beginnings, would envy such a life.

*Protégé*: Envy?

*Director*: Not in the sense of jealousy, but in the sense of admiration. But beware.

*Protégé*: Of what?

*Director*: Some understand that a single beginning is a great prize. And they force themselves into an ill-fitting beginning in hopes of winning that prize. That is a very, very foolish thing.

*Protégé*: What happens to them?

*Director*: Basically? They waste their lives.

*Protégé*: I won't do that.

*Director*: Good.


~ WASTE


*Director*: But here's a criticism you might face.

*Protégé*: I'm ready. Tell me.

*Director*: Sitting by your oasis is a waste of time.

*Protégé*: Well, that's just foolish. It's never a waste to enjoy yourself.

*Director*: You surprise me with your defense.

*Protégé*: Why? You don't think it's true?

*Director*: No, I do think it's true. But it will open you to further attack.

*Protégé*: By those who do violence to enjoyment.

*Director*: Yes. Why do you think they do?

*Protégé*: Because they're jealous.

*Director*: It's that simple?

*Protégé*: Of course it is.

*Director*: Would they be jealous if you invited them to your oasis?

*Protégé*: They'd never accept the invitation.

*Director*: Why not?

*Protégé*: Because to do so would cut against the grain of their lives.

*Director*: Lives they haven't enjoyed.

*Protégé*: Yes.

*Director*: I think it would take real courage for someone like that to accept your invitation.

*Protégé*: Are you just saying that?

*Director*: No, I would admire someone for making that choice.

*Protégé*: Is that because enjoyment in life often comes down to luck, and they have had bad luck?

*Director*: I think there's some truth in that.

*Protégé*: And who can be blamed for their luck?

*Director*: Exactly.

*Protégé*: So their life up until now, it wasn't a waste, devoid of enjoyment though it was.

*Director*: Why not?

*Protégé*: Because no one likes not to enjoy. So they must have been fighting a painful battle.

*Director*: I don't know, *Protégé*. Maybe the battle they've been fighting is against us and our friends.

*Protégé*: Maybe. But we can welcome an enemy with a change of heart.

*Director*: We certainly can.

*Protégé*: But I think we need to be very careful in what we say to a person like this.

*Director*: Why?

*Protégé*: Because it would be mean to remind them of their former life.

*Director*: Then maybe we just admire them from afar. Or, then again, maybe we admire them like we would wild animals in a zoo.

*Protégé*: Sure, but we can't rattle their cage.

*Director*: Oh, a little teasing is alright. And it's even for the good.

*Protégé*: How is it good?

*Director*: They know we're honest with them this way. And to someone who's spent much of their life attacking reason, this honesty is somehow sweet.

*Protégé*: Bitter sweet.

*Director*: Yes, but they've always had the bitterness. So now they're glad for the sweet.


### ~ Sweet

*Protégé*: We've been saying that reason is sweet. Is it really?

*Director*: To those who approach it with an open heart, despite everything else in the world? It's sweet.

*Protégé*: Does reason forgive our transgressions?

*Director*: Against reason? Reason couldn't care less. The only one to forgive such transgressions is you.

*Protégé*: Reason is indestructible.

*Director*: Maybe. But those who listen to reason aren't.

*Protégé*: What if the enemy kills us all off?

*Director*: Maybe someday someone will stumble upon reason, and we'll start all over again.

*Protégé*: Someone dying of thirst in the desert.

*Director*: Sure, someone like that. Or maybe some prince living a life of stresses and pleasures. It's hard to say.

*Protégé*: What exactly is sweet about reason?

*Director*: Exactly? Oh, *Protégé*. You're compelling me to tell you about the dark side, too.

*Protégé*: There's a dark side to reason?

*Director*: Yes, and it's bitter beyond belief.

*Protégé*: Who experiences reason so? Have you?

*Director*: I have.

*Protégé*: Why haven't you said anything up until now?

*Director*: Because we've been having such a nice talk.

*Protégé*: Director, I can't believe you. Tell me about the dark side of reason.

*Director*: We spoke lightly of turning our world upside down. What isn't light is when you see that reason wants you to turn your world upside down— but you find you can't.

*Protégé*: So it's not really reason that's bitter. It's the fact that you can't comply.

*Director*: Yes.

*Protégé*: But we have to do whatever it takes!

*Director*: Of course. But what if reason shows you your world, and your world is beyond repair?

*Protégé*: Nonsense. You start with what you can, and seek to change the rest.

*Director*: That's good policy. But there are two types of 'world'. There's our individual sphere, and there's the larger sphere. What if you're called to turn both upside down?

*Protégé*: It makes no difference. You start with your own then work on the rest.

*Director*: And what if your 'rest' is this? Each time you, as a therapist, help convert one to the cause, a million go the other way. That's the world that reason shows is yours.

*Protégé*: Is it really that bad?

*Director*: It often seems that way to me.

*Protégé*: Are you a defeatist?

*Director*: Ha!

*Protégé*: Why do you laugh?

*Director*: Because that's emphatically not what I am. Remember, I fight.

*Protégé*: Against impossible odds. So you can't fight this fight alone. You need every fighter you can get. And yet you humor me with my kittens.

*Director*: Kittens grow into cats. And cats know full well how to fight.

*Protégé*: You'd put me in the front line.

*Director*: Aren't you already there?

*Protégé*: Do you find the front line sweet?

*Director*: Shall I tell you it's bitter?

*Protégé*: I don't think it's bitter with you. Talk of bitterness is just a disguise.

*Director*: What am I disguising?

*Protégé*: Your lust for the fight.

*Director*: Why would I disguise that? Shouldn't that win me praise?

*Protégé*: Yes, but then reason doesn't seem so innocent... and sweet.


## ~ Innocence


*Director*: What is innocence?

*Protégé*: Absence of guilt.

*Director*: Do you think I'm guilty in my fight?

*Protégé*: For fighting the violent? No.

*Director*: So I'm innocent?

*Protégé*: You might be innocent, but you're not an innocent.

*Director*: What does that mean?

*Protégé*: You have certain kinds of knowledge.

*Director*: Knowledge of wrong?

*Protégé*: Yes.

*Director*: How do you think I came to have such knowledge?

*Protégé*: Wrong was done to you.

*Director*: And you?

*Protégé*: I think I have that knowledge, too.

*Director*: People speak of having their innocence stolen. Violence is done, and it destroys their innocence.

*Protégé*: Once our innocence is gone, what should we do?

*Director*: We need to fight.

*Protégé*: What must we fight?

*Director*: Violence in all its forms.

*Protégé*: Then we must fight to destroy, absolutely destroy—destroy everything they believe.

*Director*: And if they believe they are good?

*Protégé*: We destroy that belief in them.

*Director*: And if they believe they are untouchable by the likes of us?

*Protégé*: We scale their city walls and destroy them in their sleep.

*Director*: You're sounding rather passionate here.

*Protégé*: Do you think that's bad?

*Director*: I think if you want to achieve your destructive goals, a calm reasoned approach is best.

*Protégé*: Why is it best?

*Director*: Because it's most likely to succeed.

*Protégé*: Is that always the reason to be gentle and sweet? Success?

*Director*: Can you think of a better reason?

*Protégé*: I can't. But it somehow seems... mercenary.

*Director*: Mercenaries can be very good fighters.

*Protégé*: I don't want to be a mercenary.

*Director*: What do you want to be?

*Protégé*: A patriot.

*Director*: Where do the kittens fit in?

*Protégé*: I think we can have more than one metaphor. Do you agree?

*Director*: We can have as many metaphors as we like. But it's best not to be too distracted by them. We might forget what we're about.

*Protégé*: And you're about war.

*Director*: And you're about play. There's need in this world for both.

*Protégé*: But your thing is so much more... serious.

*Director*: And maybe I need it because I'm less serious than you.

*Protégé*: I need play because I'm serious at heart?

*Director*: It works out well that way, don't you think?

*Protégé*: So I'm actually more of a fighter than you?

*Director*: I'm a lover. What can I say?


~ LOVERS


*Protégé*: How many lovers have you had?

*Director*: Excuse me?

*Protégé*: Oh, don't fake modesty. How many?

*Director*: More than one and less than you think.

*Protégé*: Yes, but you know I'm not talking about physical lovers. How many mental or spiritual lovers have you had?

*Director*: Not as many as those I've loved.

*Protégé*: Why do you think it's that way?

*Director*: Because I seem weird and it scares them away.

*Protégé*: You mean that seriously?

*Director*: Why would I lie?

*Protégé*: Maybe you need to seem less weird.

*Director*: Divorce myself from reason?

*Protégé*: No, but put on an act until you get close.

*Director*: And then I'll scare them away? But you're an expert here?

*Protégé*: No, I'm no expert. I always seem weird.

*Director*: Then we should help each other out.

*Protégé*: That's what we're doing with my potential friend. You're helping me, but I'm also helping you.

*Director*: How so?

*Protégé*: You might become very good friends with him.

*Director*: You think I'll love him as a true human, dedicated to reason?

*Protégé*: Who's the true human? You or him? Regardless, if he's not dedicated to reason he might at least be a fellow traveler.

*Director*: Fellow travelers aren't bad.

*Protégé*: Of course they're not.

*Director*: But they don't really win my love. It takes someone looking for the core.

*Protégé*: You don't love those who have already found the core?

*Director*: I do. But even when found we still must seek.

*Protégé*: Point taken. Reason is strange that way. But now something occurs to me. Is your army a sort of Sacred Band of Thebes, fighting out of love for each other?

*Director*: Love, in the end, is why we fight. Though I'm not sure I'd compare us to that Ancient Greek unit.

*Protégé*: Reason isn't the reason you fight?

*Director*: Reason doesn't care about fighting. People who listen to reason do.

*Protégé*: Will a fight from love always win over a fight from hate?

*Director*: All things equal? Yes.

*Protégé*: But things are never equal, are they?

*Director*: Not in my experience, no. That's why the world is the way it is.

*Protégé*: So we'll never know victory.

*Director*: Victory isn't what you think.

*Protégé*: What is it?

*Director*: Winning another to the cause.

*Protégé*: And that's it?

*Director*: That's all it takes. As long as there is one, the cause can't die.

*Protégé*: That's the victory? Keeping the cause alive?

*Director*: Protégé, what more do you expect?


## ~ MORE


*Protégé*: I want the cause to thrive!

*Director*: Then let's convert fifty million at once.

*Protégé*: Be serious. We can't convert that many.

*Director*: True. We can't convert even one.

*Protégé*: Why not?

*Director*: We're not converting. We're helping people see what they are.

*Protégé*: We're a sort of mirror? Nothing more?

*Director*: Nothing more.

*Protégé*: Even to the bad?

*Director*: Even to the violent. We're nothing more.

*Protégé*: That's the fight you fight? To hold a mirror in their face?

*Director*: That's the fight. And victory is good.

*Protégé*: You're talking about one of the violent seeing what they are.

*Director*: They see themselves and then they compare themselves to us.

*Protégé*: And when they make that comparison?

*Director*: Sometimes? They lose their confidence and go quietly away.

*Protégé*: Can they take up reason?

*Director*: That's not who they are.

*Protégé*: That sounds like a very sad life.

*Director*: Would you rather we didn't fight the war?

*Protégé*: No. There are casualties in war. We have to accept that fact.

*Director*: Oh, I accepted that fact a while ago. Are you sure you accept it now?

*Protégé*: You can see I still have my doubts.

*Director*: You don't really believe there are different kinds of people in the world. It's a democratic thing. Everyone is equal; everyone is the same.

*Protégé*: Maybe that is what I believe.

*Director*: Then everything we've said just falls apart.

*Protégé*: No, not everything. We still value reason the same.

*Director*: And when those who reason fall prey to violent attack? What then? 'Oh, they just need to come around and they'll stop attacking us. We're really all the same.' No, we're not.

*Protégé*: Is it philosophical to be categorical that way? To talk in absolutes?

*Director*: Is it philosophical to be crucified by a belief that we're somehow all the same? What more do you need? What do you want?

*Protégé*: I want…. I don't know what I want. What do you want?

*Director*: Conversations that touch on the core.

*Protégé*: That's really all you want?

*Director*: I want victories, sure. But what I really want is to talk with those who listen. Because I—for my part—listen, too.

*Protégé*: In other words, you want friends.

*Director*: Yes.

*Protégé*: That's what I want.

*Director*: Just promise me one thing.

*Protégé*: What?

*Director*: Don't make friends with the enemy.

*Protégé*: I won't. But I want to know why not.

*Director*: Because to do so you must stop being what you are. And then you're as good as dead.

## ~ Death, Again

*Protégé*: Now I understand why you have so many new beginnings.

*Director*: Why is that?

*Protégé*: Because you attempt to make friends with people, and then you realize they're really not in touch with reason, and so you break things off. And then you start again.

*Director*: I never doubted you were a very perceptive person. But then what happens with the person who makes only one beginning, one friend, and takes it all the way to the end?

*Protégé*: I think that person is lucky.

*Director*: Isn't it better to have more than one friend?

*Protégé*: I don't know. If it's a really good friend? Maybe not. Maybe one is all we need. It's like what you said about keeping the cause alive. One is all it takes.

*Director*: What happens if your friend dies?

*Protégé*: I think you fade away into death yourself. Life just isn't the same.

*Director*: Not even if you're devoted to reason?

*Protégé*: Reason can say it's time to die.

*Director*: I don't like this much.

*Protégé*: Why not?

*Director*: I'm looking for fighters for the cause.

*Protégé*: Then let me ask you this. If the fight is real, what's the risk?

*Director*: What do you mean? We're subject to violent attack.

*Protégé*: Yes, but can it be only with words?

*Director*: It can be yes, of course. But it can also be with the full panoply of violence's awful ways. I thought we were clear on this.

*Protégé*: Just to be sure, we might be beaten to death or shot and killed?

*Director*: Certainly, yes—under the right circumstances. Are you having second thoughts?

*Protégé*: Somehow this is all becoming much more real. I know I can handle the words. But the rest of it? I can't handle that the way you can, *Director*.

*Director*: I'm afraid too, *Protégé*. But I'm aware that everything is at stake. And so I try.

*Protégé*: Yes, but when the violent are stirred they get very upset. And they get especially upset if we persuade their young toward reason. I'm very afraid of that, so I can't take it too far.

*Director*: Not even with your potential friend?

*Protégé*: There's something you don't know.

*Director*: Oh?

*Protégé*: His father is a Russian mafia don.

*Director*: How do you know?

*Protégé*: Everyone knows. Does it change how we interact with him?

*Director*: Not necessarily. But it will influence certain tactical things.

*Protégé*: Tactical things?

*Director*: Examples we give to make things clear, for instance. Minor things like that.

*Protégé*: That's really it?

*Director*: Well, who he is shapes how he'll respond to us. Knowing some of his background facts might help us understand why he reacts the way he does. But we have to be careful here.

*Protégé*: Why?

*Director*: We can choke on those facts—and die.


## ~ FACTS


*Protégé*: Aren't you being a little dramatic here? Why would we choke on a fact?

*Director*: The fact might challenge one of our beliefs. When that happens we must either somehow reconcile the two, reject the fact, or reject the belief.

*Protégé*: So if we fail to reject either of them, and can't reconcile the two, we choke.

*Director*: Yes. And, in a way, it speaks well of us when we do.

*Protégé*: When we choke? I don't understand.

*Director*: Let's say the fact goes against a belief, an important belief. We don't want to reject the belief. But something in us accepts the truth of the fact. That's what speaks well. And we try to reconcile the two. This leads to all sorts of trouble if the fact and belief really can't be reconciled.

*Protégé*: What kind of trouble?

*Director*: Mental gymnastics like you wouldn't believe.

*Protégé*: Oh, I've seen some very strange opinions and theories about those opinions.

*Director*: Yes. But the choking happens because we never fully swallow the fact. It's like tasting a piece of meat, savoring it even, but failing to chew it up.

*Protégé*: And the meat might kill you for it.

*Director*: Yes. It's impossible to chew something that's stuck in your throat. And that's what's sad about this whole affair. We realize too late we should have chewed. But now there's nothing we can do.

*Protégé*: I don't believe it happens like that.

*Director*: You believe we can always chew?

*Protégé*: Yes. The metaphor is no good. Well, maybe it's good to give us an idea. But overall it fails to describe things adequately.

*Director*: Then let's drop all metaphor and speak in simple, clear terms. What happens when we don't accept a fact?

*Protégé*: We try to prove it isn't a fact.

*Director*: And if reason says it's a fact? And reasoned people agree?

*Protégé*: We appeal to those who do violence to reason.

*Director*: We call on them to do violence to the fact.

*Protégé*: Yes, precisely.

*Director*: How do they do violence to the fact?

*Protégé*: They deny its basis.

*Director*: And this can take so many forms?

*Protégé*: So many, yes. But the deniers have one great advantage.

*Director*: Tell me what it is.

*Protégé*: They don't have to make a very good case.

*Director*: Why not?

*Protégé*: Because there are many who want to see the fact go away. Any case, however pathetic or weak, it causes them to exclaim, 'There! It's shown to general satisfaction that it's no fact at all! Just wishful thinking by some of the pansies!'

*Director*: Pansies?

*Protégé*: Substitute whatever word you like that suggests we're weak.

*Director*: Okay, I understand what you mean. And I take your point. But it's no less a fact for all that.

*Protégé*: That's absolutely true. But what's wrong? Why do you seem strange?

*Director*: There are facts, and then there are 'facts'. I seem strange because I almost forgot—we live, largely, in a world of 'facts'.

*Protégé*: And that's part of our fight. To clear up the facts.

*Director*: I think you may have found your fight.

*Protégé*: I'd be more than willing to fight for facts.

*Director*: That's good. I think you'll do well. But what about your therapy job?

*Protégé*: Job? It's a calling. I'd fight for facts within the job. Facts that others need to accept.

*Director*: I think you'll do quite well.

*Protégé*: Thank you. But what about you? Are facts a part of your fight?

*Director*: No doubt they are. But I use them as weapons to kill.


~ KILLING


*Protégé*: Why is it always killing with you?

*Director*: Oh, it's just my dominant metaphor. We can talk about it in another way, if you like that better.

*Protégé*: I would like that better.

*Director*: Well, I seize on a fact and press it home as a point until I puncture the bladder of the violent in nature.

*Protégé*: The bladder that keeps them afloat?

*Director*: Yes. Do you take my point?

*Protégé*: I do. But don't press it too hard!

*Director*: I would never press it with you.

*Protégé*: Not even if I rejected a life-giving fact?

*Director*: It's not in your nature. You never would except under duress. And I would kill those who would put you under duress.

*Protégé*: How are you so confident in your ability to 'kill'?

*Director*: I've killed many before.

*Protégé*: What does killing really involve?

*Director*: Stopping the violent attacks.

*Protégé*: When someone stops, what do they do?

*Director*: They go out to pasture and reflect on their ill spent life.

*Protégé*: I can get comfortable with that.

*Director*: That's good. It's really not such a bad fate, you know.

*Protégé*: No, it's not.

*Director*: But do you agree these people differ from you and me in something very important?

*Protégé*: This is the fact you want me to accept.

*Director*: The fact that you're calling it a fact is heartening. Is it a fact?

*Protégé*: It is. But here's the thing.

*Director*: Oh, no.

*Protégé*: Just listen. It is a fact that these people are different. But it might not have to have been that way. Do you know what I mean?

*Director*: I'm afraid I do. Could have been. Might have been. That's what the ones I kill spend their days thinking about. You're not one of them.

*Protégé*: You want me to focus on what is.

*Director*: What else would you focus on? Do you know what I mean?

*Protégé*: Reason is about the is.

*Director*: Yes, that's true. How can you know this truth and yet reject the facts?

*Protégé*: I'm young.

*Director*: That's no excuse. I have many more years than you, but I, too, am young. You don't see me rejecting any facts.

*Protégé*: Only 'facts'.

*Director*: Yes. And I reject them with extreme prejudice.

*Protégé*: That's just something people say. You don't have any prejudices. Do you?

*Director*: Thank you for catching me in my nonsense. I like to think I have no prejudices. But promise me you'll tell me if I do.

*Protégé*: What if you'd kill me for it?

*Director*: Then my entire life would have been a waste.

*Protégé*: Then I feel secure enough to say what I think. And if I think you have a prejudice, I will tell you.

*Director*: Thank you, from the bottom of my heart.

## ~ LEARNING

*Protégé*: Do you learn from those you kill?

*Director*: The dead have much to teach.

*Protégé*: Is that why you read old philosophers?

*Director*: Who says they're dead?

*Protégé*: They live on in their works?

*Director*: Yes.

*Protégé*: What work will you live on in?

*Director*: I don't care much about that. I'm different from the others this way.

*Protégé*: I want a legacy with my clients. I want to make a name for myself.

*Director*: You want to be famous?

*Protégé*: Famous among those who know. Don't you want fame like this?

*Director*: It's better than general fame. But I don't love winning fame.

*Protégé*: What do you love?

*Director*: I love to learn.

*Protégé*: You learn from the living; you learn from the dead?

*Director*: And those in-between.

*Protégé*: What's in-between living and dead?

*Director*: There are many sorts of weird creatures who hover between life and death.

*Protégé*: Weird means touched by reason?

*Director*: Touched, yes—but only touched.

*Protégé*: I imagine most people are this way.

*Director*: Yes, that's so. Most people are touched, in one way or another—when times are good.

*Protégé*: How are times now?

*Director*: I think they're pretty good, for now.

*Protégé*: How quickly can they change?

*Director*: How quickly can the violent organize themselves?

*Protégé*: That's up to the living and those in-between.

*Director*: So you can see why it's good to win over as many in-betweens as we can.

*Protégé*: Win them over to the cause, yes. But are we just showing them the mirror?

*Director*: Yes. But I don't want to mislead you here. These people aren't fully alive.

*Protégé*: They're partly alive. And that can't change?

*Director*: They are what they are. That cannot change. Do we disagree here? Are you still stuck on this fact?

*Protégé*: I don't know if it's a fact. If you're partly alive, why can't you become fully alive?

*Director*: Because you're actually dead but seem alive through true opinion.

*Protégé*: You're scaring me a little. Is the world really so bad? Is it really full of the seemingly alive?

*Director*: Tell me, *Protégé*. What was your earliest dream?

*Protégé*: What?

*Director*: What was your earliest dream?

*Protégé*: I was all alone in a deserted city, being chased by a giant monster. What was yours?

*Director*: I was all alone in a city full of mannequins, frozen people. I went everywhere I could, but it was always the same. Not a living soul to be found.


~ CITIES


*Protégé*: The dreams are similar. What do you think they mean?

*Director*: I don't know.

*Protégé*: Maybe they just mean we're alive, and all the living share a similar dream.

*Director*: Again, I don't know.

*Protégé*: But surely there's something important and special about similarities in earliest dreams.

*Director*: What do you think these similarities mean? The ones who dreamed them were born to fight for the cause?

*Protégé*: Yes. Is there any other conclusion?

*Director*: I can't think of what it might be. We were alone and afraid. The only way to overcome the loneliness and fear is... to fight.

*Protégé*: But I couldn't fight that monster.

*Director*: And what point was there in fighting the mannequins?

*Protégé*: So the dreams are only a prelude.

*Director*: Prelude to the fight?

*Protégé*: I don't know. Maybe there's something else.

*Director*: I'd be grateful if you could say what.

*Protégé*: Well, my monster. Maybe I should have turned and confronted him. Maybe we could have been friends.

*Director*: I don't know about that.

*Protégé*: And your mannequins. You said they were frozen people. Maybe if you warmed them up you could have had some friends.

*Director*: Maybe. But why do you think we both dreamed of deserted cities?

*Protégé*: The nuclear threat?

*Director*: But my city wasn't destroyed. It was just barren. Devoid of life. And yours?

*Protégé*: The same.

*Director*: And why did you have a monster and I had mannequins?

*Protégé*: I don't know.

*Director*: Do people in other parts of the world have dreams like this?

*Protégé*: Maybe it's not so uncommon.

*Director*: Maybe. I don't know if that's good or bad.

*Protégé*: Still, they're only dreams.

*Director*: But maybe we process things in dreams we don't or can't process in ordinary life.

*Protégé*: I'll make a point of asking my clients what their earliest dreams were. I won't share with you who dreamed what, but I'll tell you if there's a theme among the living.

*Director*: Good. I'd like to know.

*Protégé*: I find that remarkable.

*Director*: What?

*Protégé*: That I can help you know.

*Director*: Don't sell yourself short. You're a remarkable human being—which is to say you're alive. And that's all that counts with me.


~ ALIVE


*Protégé*: You set the bar low.

*Director*: Then try to be fully alive. That's what I aim to achieve for myself. But there is so much violence in the world. It makes this goal the greatest challenge there can be.

*Protégé*: You really mean it? Being wholly alive is the most difficult thing in the world?

*Director*: I really mean it. And I think your monster says it all. You were alive in your dream. The monster wanted to destroy you. Or have I got it wrong?

*Protégé*: No, you're absolutely right. Somehow I knew, knew to a certainty—I couldn't let that monster get me.

*Director*: How do you think you knew?

*Protégé*: Children can pick up on all the violence in the world. They intuit that it's bad.

*Director*: And then it comes out in their dreams. No escape.

*Protégé*: But there must be something they can do.

*Director*: While dreaming?

*Protégé*: No, in real life.

*Director*: They can resist.

*Protégé*: And be punished for every little bit of resistance.

*Director*: Maybe that helps them grow strong.

*Protégé*: Or breaks them irreversibly.

*Director*: Did your monster get you?

*Protégé*: No, I was always able to hide.

*Director*: That's good—provided you didn't lose yourself in the process.

*Protégé*: Do you think I did?

*Director*: It's hard to say.

*Protégé*: Sometimes I think I've lost myself. Do you ever feel that way?

*Director*: Yes.

*Protégé*: Well, I'd like to help others find themselves—me included!

*Director*: Others who had to hide? I think you'll find satisfaction in that.

*Protégé*: I think I will, too.

*Director*: You'll show them they're not the only ones alive.

*Protégé*: I'll hold the mirror up and show them the fog of our breath. I'll simply demonstrate that we're alive.

*Director*: And they'll pay you for this.

*Protégé*: I would do it for free.

*Director*: Yes, but you have to live. Can you accept the fact that you have to live?

*Protégé*: Yes, but not if they can't afford it.

*Director*: That's fine. But for those who can afford it, are you okay with that?

*Protégé*: I am.

*Director*: That's good.

*Protégé*: Yes, but *Director*, what about you?

*Director*: What about me?

*Protégé*: You're looking for life in a corporation. Aren't you bound to fail?

*Director*: I see you like to tease.

*Protégé*: Ha, ha. But really, can't you look someplace better?

*Director*: Well, we touched on this before. I have my fight, and my friends. Between the two I'm doing alright.

*Protégé*: But what really keeps you alive? The fight?

*Director*: Love.

*Protégé*: You love the fight.

*Director*: I love the people engaged in the fight.

*Protégé*: If they're already engaged in the fight, what do they need from you?

*Director*: In a serious fight, reinforcements never hurt.

*Protégé*: True.

*Director*: Or do they?

*Protégé*: Why would you ask that?

*Director*: Because I'm not sure.

*Protégé*: How can reinforcement hurt?

*Director*: It might interfere with someone who is fighting quite well on their own. It might cause them to lose their edge, their focus, their point.

*Protégé*: Well then, I'll give you a good rule of thumb.

*Director*: Please.

*Protégé*: When in doubt, help. You can always stop if you come to see they're okay on their own. And that, *Director*, is our only law of war. We must try to help when we can.

*Director*: All else goes?

*Protégé*: Yes.

*Director*: Protégé, I like your style.


~ STYLE


*Protégé*: Violence is some people's style.

*Director*: Live by the sword, die by the sword.

*Protégé*: I'm not sure I'd like to die that way. How about you?

*Director*: That's the way I'd like to go.

*Protégé*: Why?

*Director*: It's in keeping with my life.

*Protégé*: And how will I die? Like a rabbit?

*Director*: Running until you're caught? There's nothing wrong with that.

*Protégé*: You really mean it? Rabbits can die in style?

*Director*: Of course they can. Each living creature has its own best style of death.

*Protégé*: What about those you put to death?

*Director*: Who says they were ever alive?

*Protégé*: Alright, point taken.

*Director*: You seem to begrudge the point. Still not accepting the fact?

*Protégé*: No, I accept the fact alright. That doesn't mean I have to like it.

*Director*: Fair enough. But tell me, is listening to reason a sort of style?

*Protégé*: Sure. Only the cool kids do it.

*Director*: Seriously. Is it a style in the sense that violence is a style as you said?

*Protégé*: I think the actual listening isn't a style. It's something far more. But when we walk away from the core, as we all must eventually do, reason marks us with a style of our own.

*Director*: Are you saying we can't simply listen to reason forever?

*Protégé*: Of course we can't. There are pressing things in life to which we must attend.

*Director*: Okay. But what's this about individual style?

*Protégé*: The unique facts of our life, once in contact with reason, grow into a unique style of our own.

*Director*: Is it safe to say anyone who has a unique style has been in touch with reason?

*Protégé*: You're testing me now.

*Director*: I honestly want to know.

*Protégé*: Want to know what I think?

*Director*: Want to know the truth.

*Protégé*: Alright. Yes, anyone with a unique style has been in touch with reason.

*Director*: And what about the violent?

*Protégé*: No unique style for them.

*Director*: Why not?

*Protégé*: Because the violent always conform.

*Director*: To what?

*Protégé*: The greatest local force.

*Director*: Why?

*Protégé*: Because they truly know nothing better.


~ LIES


*Director*: And the unique do know something better.

*Protégé*: Of course.

*Director*: I think I'd still test them, just to make sure they really do.

*Protégé*: That's probably wise—so long as you don't drive them away with your tests.

*Director*: Oh, I'm pretty good with tests. I know how not to drive others away.

*Protégé*: I think you're lying to me.

*Director*: What am I lying about?

*Protégé*: I believe you know how not to drive people away. But I think the drift of what you said was a lie. You implied that you don't drive people away. But you do. You want them to fight on their own.

*Director*: That's true. I do. For the reasons I've already said.

*Protégé*: I wonder when you'll drive me away.

*Director*: Why would I drive you away? You'll go to fight on your own, all on your own—of your own free will.

*Protégé*: Will you visit me?

*Director*: Of course, *Protégé*. We're friends, aren't we? And have you forgotten I'll be a client?

*Protégé*: Tell me. Do you ever visit those you've driven away?

*Director*: I have.

*Protégé*: How did it go?

*Director*: Suffice it to say it was strange.

*Protégé*: Do you mean you were like strangers?

*Director*: That's an excellent question. The answer is a qualified yes.

*Protégé*: Why a qualified yes?

*Director*: Because we knew each other so well. But now we were in very different places.

*Protégé*: The circumstances changed.

*Director*: Yes. And to attempt to act as though nothing had changed, that would be a lie. Much and little had changed at once. How do you talk about that?

*Protégé*: I think I understand.

*Director*: Besides, I didn't meet with them alone.

*Protégé*: Why not?

*Director*: We needed a reminder of our roles in life.

*Protégé*: That I don't understand. You're a sort of actor?

*Director*: All of us who act in life are actors. I act. I wear the guise of a fighter—and I fight. So I brought with me someone who only knows me as a fighter.

*Protégé*: As a reminder of what you are.

*Director*: Yes.

*Protégé*: Why was that necessary?

*Director*: Because I wasn't always such a fighter for the cause.

*Protégé*: And your old friend knew you before the cause?

*Director*: Right. We knew each other before the beginnings of our fight.

*Protégé*: You knew me before the beginning of my fight. But I guess I'm not worried, since you say you won't drive me away. But does that mean I'm not worth driving away?

*Director*: Only you would ask. Of course not. It just means some of our circumstances in life allow us to be together with others; other circumstances force us apart.

*Protégé*: And you press to the limit what allows you to be together, in order to make a friend.

*Director*: To the absolute limit, yes.

*Protégé*: I think I can understand. And when you're pressing it to the limit, you push truthfulness that way, too?

*Director*: That's exactly the limit I have in mind. I can't go farther than I can allow myself in truth.

*Protégé*: What does that mean? There are things you can't say?

*Director*: Do you have things you can't say?

*Protégé*: I have things I don't want to say. That's different, isn't it?

*Director*: Very. I have things I don't like to say. But I also have things I cannot say. I'll say the former to my friend, but not the latter. This can create a sort of friction.

*Protégé*: I can see how. So you only push them away when the friction gets too bad?

*Director*: When it gets too bad they often leave on their own.

*Protégé*: I'm afraid something like this will happen to me in my professional life.

*Director*: People will be open with you but only so far?

*Protégé*: Yes, and then they'll simply go away.

*Director*: Maybe you should want them to go, go and stand on their own two feet. After all, who wants to be in therapy forever?

*Protégé*: That's a good point. And who wants their clients to stay with them forever?

*Director*: Someone with the wrong motivation.

## ~ Motivation

*Protégé*: Agreed. But what should motivate us? Love?

*Director*: Love, certainly.

*Protégé*: What else?

*Director*: Happiness.

*Protégé*: You find happiness in the fight?

*Director*: I do, even when it's very hard.

*Protégé*: How do you achieve that?

*Director*: I love what I do.

*Protégé*: It's really that simple?

*Director*: Don't worry; you'll find out. Therapy will be a battle, you know. A very hard battle at times. And you'll find that you're happy in the fight.

*Protégé*: I hope so. How can you tell?

*Director*: I have long experience in these things.

*Protégé*: Well, thanks.

*Director*: For what?

*Protégé*: Having confidence in me.

*Director*: There's no need for thanks. The light of reason showed this truth about you. Do we thank the sun for shining on us? No. The sun wants no thanks.

*Protégé*: How modest of you to compare yourself to the sun!

*Director*: But all of us, those fighting violence for the cause, we all are suns. We all are stars in the sky.

*Protégé*: Can we fight violence without the cause?

*Director*: Why would we? What would be our motivation?

*Protégé*: Ethics?

*Director*: That's a thin reed. What else?

*Protégé*: Professionalism?

*Director*: Really? That's enough to carry us through the fight of our lives?

*Protégé*: So the cause of gentle reason is really the only true motivation.

*Director*: Yes.

*Protégé*: Not many people are gentle, *Director*.

*Director*: I've noticed. But the ones who are can be very, very strong.

*Protégé*: Gentle strength.

*Director*: Exactly. Some of them are figuring battles we didn't even know exist. That's how gentle they are.

*Protégé*: You mean they're fighting and all the while they seem to us to be engaged in no fight?

*Director*: That's what I mean.

*Protégé*: Are you saying they're gentle to the enemy?

*Director*: When they can be, yes. It's a paradox. The best way to fight violence is through gentle, relentless strength.

*Protégé*: Remorseless strength?

*Director*: Gentle, relentless, remorseless strength.

*Protégé*: I need some work on the remorseless part.

*Director*: It takes time. You need to learn that your cause is—

*Protégé*: Just? I know my cause is just.

*Director*: So why do you feel remorse?

*Protégé*: Habit.

*Director*: That's a very fine answer, *Protégé*. Habits take time to change. You're lucky.

*Protégé*: Why am I lucky?

*Director*: You have time.

*Protégé*: I have more than time.

*Director*: What have you got?

*Protégé*: Motivation.


- TIME


*Director*: Time is something the violent never seem to have.

*Protégé*: It's true. They always put pressure on you to decide things at once.

*Director*: Why do you think that is?

*Protégé*: They don't want you to have time to think.

*Director*: Does thinking take much time?

*Protégé*: If you're trying to think things through? Yes.

*Director*: What would make you think you need to think things through?

*Protégé*: It's just a feeling you get when you're rushed.

*Director*: Thinking relies on a feeling to know when it's time to think?

*Protégé*: Yes, I think so. While thought and feeling are different things, they're closely related.

*Director*: But doesn't feeling sometimes overwhelm thought?

*Protégé*: True.

*Director*: But sometimes thought overcomes feeling.

*Protégé*: Can you give an example?

*Director*: Let's say you were embarrassed to say thought depends on a feeling. Embarrassment is a feeling. Do you agree?

*Protégé*: I do.

*Director*: If you think enough about the truth of what you said about feeling, your good thoughts will overcome your embarrassment. You'll feel embarrassed no more. But you have to allot yourself plenty of time. Some feelings are very strong.

*Protégé*: Maybe that's why there's a stigma attached to spending lots of thoughtful time alone.

*Director*: I'm not following.

*Protégé*: Sorry, I should explain. There are people who like it when people like me are embarrassed.

*Director*: Why?

*Protégé*: It's a sort of violence to thought.

*Director*: Embarrassment?

*Protégé*: Yes, you can't think in front of those who embarrass you. You have to go off on your own and think. But the violent ones don't like that. They fear that if you have time, you'll think things through.

*Director*: Why are they afraid of that?

*Protégé*: Because you'll see them for what they are.

*Director*: Do they know what they are?

*Protégé*: I don't know. Maybe some of them do, the leaders.

*Director*: So what if you see?

*Protégé*: If I can see, I can press a point—and pop the bladder that keeps them afloat.

*Director*: Bladders are hollow. What makes them hollow?

*Protégé*: The reasons of the violent are only on the surface. Our reasons run all the way through.

*Director*: Hmm.

*Protégé*: What 'hmm'?

*Director*: I'm just not so sure that some of the violent aren't deep.


## ~ Violence, Again

*Director*: But what do you think makes people violent in the first place?

*Protégé*: The fear of being alone with time to think. Everything follows from that. It's the seed of the rebellion against reason. What do you think?

*Director*: Have you ever been afraid of being alone with time to think?

*Protégé*: Never. Have you?

*Director*: No. But I don't think we can accept this as a rule, this thinking about what makes people violent.

*Protégé*: Why not?

*Director*: Because there might be those who fear being alone who don't turn violent. They stay scared and they're relieved when they're with others again.

*Protégé*: Of course. Rabbits. But let's describe those who turn violent. What really happens there?

*Director*: Well, if it's as you say, this fear causes them to do violence to their own reason within.

*Protégé*: And then?

*Director*: They come to fear those who aren't afraid to be alone—and they lash out against them, much as they lashed out within. How's that?

*Protégé*: Good. I think it's true. And I'm starting to take your point.

*Director*: Which point?

*Protégé*: The one that says people are what they are and that's really all we can know. At a certain point we have to say, 'This is the way you are.' And then we leave it at that.

*Director*: Don't therapists try to get behind the-way-you-are and find out why you are that way?

*Protégé*: Many do. But I fail to see the point. Better to show them very clearly what they are, then see if there's a way to change for the better.

*Director*: But if people are what they are, what can change?

*Protégé*: They can either make themselves more of what they are, or less.

*Director*: Will you take on violent clients?

*Protégé*: And make them more violent? You already know the answer here. I'll only take on the gentle—and maybe one or two of the violent, as you recommend. But I won't let the violent be more of what they are.

*Director*: How do you make the gentle more of what they are?

*Protégé*: I'll tell them they have beauty in them, and they should bring more of it out.

*Director*: Will you teach them to fight?

*Protégé*: In self-defense? I will.

*Director*: What if they don't want to fight? What if they want to just run back to their hole?

*Protégé*: I'll share your metaphor with them. They aren't just letting themselves down if they go back in the hole. They're letting all of us down.

*Director*: Can you be a whole human being if you don't learn to fight?

*Protégé*: No, I don't think you can. And that holds even if your metaphor is playful kittens.

*Director*: Is my metaphor somehow controlling? In other words, does my metaphor best describe the scene?

*Protégé*: I think it does. It's a war out there. Truly, in a very real sense. But there are also times when we should play. After all, what's the point of the war if all we do is fight? We're fighting for something, right?

*Director*: That's a very good reminder. We can get carried away and see only the fight.

*Protégé*: Give me a few years then come to therapy with me. I'll make sure you don't get carried away.

*Director*: I'll take you up on that.

*Protégé*: And if you ever think I've come to backslide and give up on the fight, I want to know.

### ~ AWARE

*Protégé*: I wonder if my potential friend is aware of the fight.

*Director*: I think we're all aware at some level. The question is what we do about it.

*Protégé*: What can we do? I know we can take direct action. I see this in you. My action is more removed. What other action is there?

*Director*: I have a friend who writes.

*Protégé*: What does he or she write?

*Director*: He writes arguments about violence.

*Protégé*: That, too, is at a remove. It's something like what I'm doing. Helping people stand up tall and fight their fight.

*Director*: Your action seems more direct. You meet with those you'd help. And you can learn from them. My friend writes and then sends it off to goodness knows where.

*Protégé*: Is your friend a rabbit?

*Director*: More so than either you or I.

*Protégé*: Well, there's a place for rabbits in this world. I'd love to meet with him and make him a fighter.

*Director*: Oh, my friend fights. But mostly he fights the demons inside. His works are handbooks for how to win the fight against such things.

*Protégé*: So he's aware.

*Director*: Very. And sometimes he fights in person.

*Protégé*: That's good. But there's nothing wrong with indirect fire.

*Director*: Yes, and I think that describes his works well.

*Protégé*: Who reads his books? You said he sends them off to goodness knows where.

*Director*: All he knows for sure is that friends read the books. But sometimes the enemy, too.

*Protégé*: What happens then?

*Director*: He comes under attack.

*Protégé*: We need to help him here.

*Director*: Agreed.

*Protégé*: Are there other sorts of fighting friends?

*Director*: You mean ways to fight? There are as many ways to fight as there are friends of reason in this world.

*Protégé*: And you're a student of their martial arts.

*Director*: Yes. I look for every advantage I can get. And I teach those who want to learn.

*Protégé*: How do you teach?

*Director*: First, I make sure they're aware of the extent of the fight. Some people only know of the battle in their own limited world. They don't know others are fighting nearby.

*Protégé*: How does it help them to know of the others?

*Director*: It helps to know you're not all alone. Or don't you agree?

*Protégé*: No, I agree. We lend each other strength.

*Director*: Yes. So, I make them aware of the larger fight, if they don't already know. And I suggest certain techniques that might help them win.

*Protégé*: I think you're the general of the battlefield today.

*Director*: But I don't order people around. I suggest ways to fight, that's all. The rest is up to them. They have to fight on their own. We all do.

*Protégé*: Can we take breaks from the fight and enjoy each other's company?

*Director*: Play like kittens now and then? Of course. Just not as often as we might like.

*Protégé*: Will the war ever end?

*Director*: Sure—if we lose.

*Protégé*: So there's no hope?

*Director*: Of course there's hope. Hope that we'll win a fight. Hope that things will get better. Hope that we'll get the enemy under control.

*Protégé*: Has the enemy ever been under control?

*Director*: I don't know.

*Protégé*: Isn't this something we urgently need to know?

*Director*: Well, I've searched through many historical records. I never found a place where the violence was wholly under control. But I'll keep looking.

*Protégé*: So will I.


~ CONTROL


*Director*: But there's a problem here.

*Protégé*: What problem?

*Director*: When we seek to control, we are in turn controlled. Does that make any sense to you?

*Protégé*: It does, but I want to hear more.

*Director*: It takes violence to control violence.

*Protégé*: Better to kill and be done with it?

*Director*: Yes. So we kill all the violent we can.

*Protégé*: Put them out to pasture.

*Director*: Yes. Give them time to think.

*Protégé*: So we're looking for a historical period where most of the violent are dead.

*Director*: Rendered ineffective on the battlefield, yes. But here's the trick. Some of the violent are killed by the violent.

*Protégé*: So we use the violent to help us in our fight?

*Director*: You didn't hear it from me, but yes. At times it makes sense. But there's risk in this.

*Protégé*: What risk?

*Director*: Sometimes when we work with the violent, we become violent ourselves.

*Protégé*: I thought we are what we are.

*Director*: We are. But violence might become... a habit.

*Protégé*: Habits can change us.

*Director*: Slowly, but yes.

*Protégé*: Then we're really not simply what we are?

*Director*: No, we can change.

*Protégé*: So the dead out to pasture can come to reason?

*Director*: Better late than never.

*Protégé*: The world is more fluid than you let on!

*Director*: Sorry, the demands of our talk required us to see things as less fluid for a while. But do you agree?

*Protégé*: Of course I agree. The world isn't a cartoon in black and white.

*Director*: Do you remember we said there are shades of gray?

*Protégé*: We may have said it, but we didn't emphasize it. But I think I understand why we didn't. We were exaggerating to make a point.

*Director*: That point made, do we have to go back now and rethink all we said?

*Protégé*: I think we do. But let's save that for another time. I don't think I have the strength to do it today.

*Director*: Sounds good to me. But, really, there isn't much to rethink. So go back and do this as soon as you can. I don't want our old, limited view to occupy the place of our new fuller view for long.

*Protégé*: Fuller view? There's more?

*Director*: There's always more. You have to get used to reasoning, friend.

*Protégé*: I've reasoned plenty on my own. But this is somehow more demanding. Why do you think that is?

*Director*: When we reason on our own we can avoid uncomfortable truths. When we reason with others, good others, that's not so easy to do.


## ~ COMFORT


*Protégé*: But shouldn't reason bring us comfort?

*Director*: That's a very important question.

*Protégé*: What's the answer?

*Director*: It's complicated.

*Protégé*: How so?

*Director*: When you think of comfort, what do you think?

*Protégé*: I think of relaxation with everything I need—warmth, food, drink, and so on.

*Director*: When you're reasoning, do you feel relaxed?

*Protégé*: If I'm reasoning about things I already know? Yes. But if I'm breaking new ground? No, I wouldn't say I feel relaxed.

*Director*: Why would you reason about things you already know?

*Protégé*: I might be explaining things to a client.

*Director*: And if the client says something new, something you've never heard?

*Protégé*: I'd reason on that.

*Director*: Could you rest until you'd reasoned it through?

*Protégé*: No, I couldn't.

*Director*: Rest and relaxation are akin, no?

*Protégé*: They are.

*Director*: And you need to be relaxed in order to be comfortable?

*Protégé*: As I said.

*Director*: So while reasoning on this new thing, you wouldn't be comfortable.

*Protégé*: Maybe that's true. But there's nowhere else I'd rather be.

*Director*: You'd choose to be uncomfortable?

*Protégé*: There really is no choice. I'd be uncomfortable either way.

*Director*: Something new, unreasoned upon, makes you uncomfortable.

*Protégé*: Yes, it does.

*Director*: So you'd reason upon all unreasoned-upon things, as far as your clients go.

*Protégé*: I would.

*Director*: Would the violent?

*Protégé*: They wouldn't.

*Director*: Why?

*Protégé*: Because they're in denial.

*Director*: Of what?

*Protégé*: They believe the discomfort of thought is greater than the discomfort of not thinking things through. They deny that thought is the better way.

*Director*: It's better because it leads us into comfort?

*Protégé*: Yes, in the end.

*Director*: Is that the goal of thought? Comfort?

*Protégé*: Of course not. Comfort is just a benefit.

*Director*: What is the goal of thought?

*Protégé*: To keep us alive.

*Director*: What's the goal of the violent? Comfort?

*Protégé*: I think it might be.

*Director*: You're not sure?

*Protégé*: Well, they don't like to think unless it's about things they already know.

*Director*: But is that really thought?

*Protégé*: No, I guess it isn't.

*Director*: Maybe we can test the violent and see if it's true that they only like to 'think' about what they already know.

*Protégé*: How can we test them?

*Director*: We'll offer them an opportunity to think about something new. Then we'll revisit them and see what progress they've made.

*Protégé*: I don't think they'll think about it at all.

*Director*: Even if it has a direct bearing on them?

*Protégé*: They'll probably just stifle the thoughts that naturally occur.

*Director*: Could you rest and relax with a stifled thought in your brain?

*Protégé*: Of course not.

*Director*: And the violent have many stifled thoughts?

*Protégé*: I think they do.

*Director*: Then maybe the violent never truly rest and relax. And, as a result, maybe they think these things are most important to them. So the effort of thought seems counter to their interests.

*Protégé*: I think that's an excellent point. We want what we haven't got.

*Director*: But we want reason. Are we saying we haven't got any?

*Protégé*: What we want is more, not any.

*Director*: That makes good sense. But does this mean we never rest?

*Protégé*: Of course not. We need to rest to give us strength to carry on.

*Director*: What do we do when we rest? Sleep?

*Protégé*: Sleep, sure. But I think we also review the things we already know.

*Director*: Why do that?

*Protégé*: Because it's comforting to do so, encouraging even. And it helps us make sure we remember.


### ~ MEMORIES


*Director*: Why do we need help remembering?

*Protégé*: Because the enemy tries to do violence to our memories.

*Director*: How do they do that?

*Protégé*: They lie and tell us we're crazy for thinking we remember what we do. 'No, that's not the way it is was! No, it couldn't have happened that way! No, you're confused!'

*Director*: I've experienced this sort of thing first hand. What can we do when confronted this way?

*Protégé*: I know what I do. I get away. I go to a safe place where I can get very clear on what I remember, and fix that memory in place.

*Director*: Then what?

*Protégé*: If I had to deal with these enemies? I don't know. What would you do?

*Director*: I'd do what you said about getting to a safe place and so on. Then I'd find ways to trip the enemy up, catch them in their lies.

*Protégé*: What good would that do?

*Director*: It would confirm to me that I'm right, that I'm not crazy. That's an important thing, *Protégé*. If this sort of thing happens to you often enough, without your proving them wrong, you might be damaged.

*Protégé*: I can see how that might happen. But I'm not good at confrontations.

*Director*: Then let me give you a tip. Confront them one at a time. The violent are strongest in a pack.

*Protégé*: That's good advice. But what do I say? You're wrong and I'm right?

*Director*: Essentially? Yes. Different circumstances will require variations on that basic theme. But that's what you have to do—stand up for yourself.

*Protégé*: And I'll grow stronger each time I do.

*Director*: Yes you will.

*Protégé*: To the point where I might be able to take on the whole group?

*Director*: Let's not get ahead of ourselves. But, yes, that might be possible. Though it's usually not a wise tactic.

*Protégé*: The violent want everything from us, our memories included. Why don't they just outright kill us?

*Director*: That's what they're trying to do. But I'll tell you a secret.

*Protégé*: What secret?

*Director*: They'd rather we kill ourselves than die at their hands.

*Protégé*: I believe it. But why do you think they want it that way? So they don't feel guilt?

*Director*: No, I think it's because they want the pleasure of breaking us, friend. To be shot down while standing tall in pride is a good way to go. They want to take that ending from us.

*Protégé*: They deserve everything we can give them.

*Director*: Will you remember this always? Or will you slide back into doubt?

*Protégé*: Only time will tell.

*Director*: A very good answer.

~ Open

*Protégé*: I'll visit the core whenever I doubt.

*Director*: Just remember to stay open when you do.

*Protégé*: I'll form a habit of openness.

*Director*: Will you stay open when you return from the core into everyday life?

*Protégé*: Should I?

*Director*: Well, here's the thing. If we stay open, can others see our reasoned learning within?

*Protégé*: I think they can.

*Director*: Both the good and the bad?

*Protégé*: I think everyone, good and bad, can see—though not everyone will know what to make of it. Or did you mean both the good learning and the bad learning?

*Director*: Do you think I meant that?

*Protégé*: No.

*Director*: Then what happens when the good and the bad see the learning inside?

*Protégé*: The good will praise and the bad will blame.

*Director*: Will the bad blame it for what it is?

*Protégé*: They'll distort what we've learned. They'll call it something else and attack.

*Director*: Do we stay open when they attack, or do we close up?

*Protégé*: I'd like to think we stay open.

*Director*: Why?

*Protégé*: Because then others can see the truth as we resist.

*Director*: Is this what you do?

*Protégé*: No, I run away.

*Director*: What's wrong with running away?

*Protégé*: There may have been more you could have done.

*Director*: And what's wrong with closing up?

*Protégé*: I'm not sure. The same?

*Director*: If you run away, there's certainly nothing more to do. Yes?

*Protégé*: At least not at that time.

*Director*: True. And if you close yourself up but stay?

*Protégé*: You might find an opportunity to open again.

*Director*: A little opening for reason?

*Protégé*: Yes.

*Director*: Should we run away from an opportunity, a chance, however small?

*Protégé*: I think it depends.

*Director*: On what?

*Protégé*: What kind of attack we're under. Haven't you heard the phrase 'live to fight another day'?

*Director*: I have. And I'm in favor of that. So I guess it's a judgment call, dependent on the forces in play. Does that sound right?

*Protégé*: It does. But it depends on one more thing.

*Director*: Oh? What?

*Protégé*: Courage.


## ~ RETREAT


*Director*: Is it more courageous to retreat than run away?

*Protégé*: If we can conduct an orderly retreat, yes. That's better.

*Director*: And when we retreat, we carry away knowledge of the enemy— because we are watchful as we retreat as opposed to turning our backs and running away.

*Protégé*: True.

*Director*: And sometimes it's not even really a retreat.

*Protégé*: What do you mean?

*Director*: Sometimes our intent is to get in, engage with the enemy, gather information, then get out., What do they call it? Reconnaissance in force?

*Protégé*: Yes, but that's something you might do. I have little force.

*Director*: Then you should conduct reconnaissance in little force, until you gain in strength.

*Protégé*: Will I gain in strength?

*Director*: Do what you intend with your clients. You'll find your strength.

*Protégé*: Are you saying I already have the strength? I just have to find it?

*Director*: People don't change. You've always had and always will have your strength.

*Protégé*: But if I've found it, I've changed.

*Director*: You'll change how you act, not who you are.

*Protégé*: But we are how we act. The violent are violent because they act violently against reason. It's the act that counts.

*Director*: True, but they can't help but act the way they act, given who they are.

*Protégé*: Do you really believe this, or is this just something you say?

*Director*: Are you asking if I don't believe in my own words?

*Protégé*: Do you?

*Director*: My words are meant to flush out knowledge. I will say whatever it takes to achieve that end.

*Protégé*: I'm not sure I like that very much.

*Director*: Why not? Are you trying to memorize my words as if they were simple truth?

*Protégé*: Why shouldn't I memorize your words? I might use them one day.

*Director*: This is the whole point. You need to come up with your own words. My words can help you uncover the words that are truly your own. But that's all. Sophists want you to memorize what they say. I don't.

*Protégé*: You want me to find my own way.

*Director*: Urgently, yes.

*Protégé*: Why urgently?

*Director*: Because the war is real and there's a very real chance we'll lose.

*Protégé*: You want me on my own front.

*Director*: I do.

*Protégé*: What happens if we lose?

*Director*: We might lose sight of the core—and never find it again.

*Protégé*: But that's why people like your friend write. They're drawing a map to the core.

*Director*: And who will have the skill required to read the map if we've lost the war?

*Protégé*: What skill does it take?

*Director*: Think of everything you've ever learned in your life. That's what it takes—and a little bit more.

~ VICTORY

*Protégé*: How do we gain the little bit more?

*Director*: By fighting the fight every day.

*Protégé*: Can we ever defeat all of the enemy and simply have peace?

*Director*: Your guess is as good as mine. But my guess is no.

*Protégé*: How would you describe victory?

*Director*: There are many ways to describe it. But here's one. Victory is when our tree bears fruit.

*Protégé*: What's your fruit? Those who ripen under your care?

*Director*: That will be your fruit, therapist. My fruits are apples from the tree of knowledge.

*Protégé*: Of course. But let's drop this metaphor.

*Director*: Do you have one better in mind?

*Protégé*: Yes. Victory for me is when a client brings me another kitten.

*Director*: I like that image. You know, thinking of your kittens at play will spur me as I fight.

*Protégé*: I thought persuasion is better than spurring.

*Director*: It is. But in the thick of it sometimes we have no choice.

*Protégé*: Agreed. But do you know what I think is strange? Here we are, all spurring ourselves to fight—and when we win, we don't celebrate the way we should.

*Director*: Why do you think we don't?

*Protégé*: We're in a terrible hurry.

*Director*: A hurry? You mean we're violent to ourselves?

*Protégé*: Yes.

*Director*: Hmm. You may have a point. I think of my friend the writer. He finishes one book and starts on another the very same day.

*Protégé*: Why do you think he does that?

*Director*: He's afraid.

*Protégé*: Of what?

*Director*: Not doing all he can.

*Protégé*: Well, if you have to be afraid of something—that's not a bad fear to have.

### ~ FEARS

*Director*: But with him it's not all fear.

*Protégé*: What is it?

*Director*: He loves the fight.

*Protégé*: The indirect fight.

*Director*: Yes, but let me share a secret with you.

*Protégé*: Please.

*Director*: He loves the direct fight more.

*Protégé*: Does he often fight the direct fight?

*Director*: No, not often anymore.

*Protégé*: Why not?

*Director*: Circumstances have brought him to the edge of the battle. He is no longer on the front line.

*Protégé*: He should go back. What stops him?

*Director*: Fame.

*Protégé*: Fame? I've never heard of your friend, have I?

*Director*: No, he has no fame.

*Protégé*: Then I don't understand.

*Director*: He thinks his work might come to be appreciated after he's dead.

*Protégé*: Why would he think that?

*Director*: It allows him not to fight the fight for fame during his life.

*Protégé*: But he wants fame?

*Director*: Yes, but he wants something else more. Victory in the fight. So he pushes fame aside and goes for the win.

*Protégé*: But then why not fight the direct fight on the front line?

*Director*: His strength lies in writing. The cause calls on us to find our strength, then use it, come what may.

*Protégé*: Fame is not his fight.

*Director*: Fame, if it comes, is a weapon to be used in the fight. He knows this. And he knows he can't control how it will be used.

*Protégé*: He's open to the come-what-may.

*Director*: Yes.

*Protégé*: I think our allies are often afraid of that.

*Director*: Afraid of what?

*Protégé*: The come-what-may.

*Director*: What do you think the come-what-may means?

*Protégé*: It means if you see you must care for the kittens, and give up the front line fight, much as you love that fight, you accept it for what it is—and take care of the cats.

*Director*: And if you realize you must give up all your clients and enter the lists?

*Protégé*: I'd be there.

*Director*: It's a sort of all but insane openness to anything, isn't it?

*Protégé*: It is. The president of a company must be open to one day serving in the kitchen, if that's what reason says.

*Director*: Reason is weird.

*Protégé*: Reason is strange.

*Director*: How do we know the president in the kitchen isn't some crackpot?

*Protégé*: We'll know by what he says and how he reacts to what we do.

*Director*: We look for the fighter in him.

*Protégé*: And we look for kitten-like play.

*Director*: Some people are very afraid, terrified, of losing their status, their place.

*Protégé*: They're cowards.

*Director*: Have you ever lost your place?

*Protégé*: Well, no.

*Director*: Then how do you know it's not to be feared?

*Protégé*: Director.

*Director*: Alright. I once worked with a 'president' in the kitchen before. He was no coward.

*Protégé*: Where was this?

*Director*: In the campus pub. He was the manager there.

*Protégé*: What was he like?

*Director*: He was wonderful. Brilliant. Happy as life can let us be. Many of his patrons loved him, and he loved them back.

*Protégé*: Sounds like he had good luck.

*Director*: Yes. But haven't you heard? We make our luck.

~ LUCK

*Protégé*: Oh, I've heard that before. I don't know that it's true.

*Director*: Maybe it's more accurate to say we make our own reactions to luck.

*Protégé*: Yes, I like that better. So how do the violent react to their bad luck?

*Director*: As you might expect. They react to it violently. They're outraged and splash violence on those nearby.

*Protégé*: And the gentle?

*Director*: They accept their luck, whatever it might be. And yes, they do try to find a way to better luck when they can. But they don't scorch the earth in the process.

*Protégé*: What is good luck, for the gentle?

*Director*: Good luck is any luck that supports a reasoned life.

*Protégé*: Bad luck is the opposite.

*Director*: Yes.

*Protégé*: So what might seem intolerable to some, to a person of reason it might seem fine.

*Director*: That's right. So be careful not to judge.

*Protégé*: I always am. In fact, I love to find these diamonds in the rough.

*Director*: You find them in rough surroundings, or the diamonds themselves are rough?

*Protégé*: Rough surroundings.

*Director*: Why do you love to find them?

*Protégé*: Because I appreciate them though they're under-appreciated.

*Director*: Are they? How do you know they're under-appreciated? Why do you make that assumption?

*Protégé*: No one there knows them for what they are.

*Director*: What are they?

*Protégé*: Gentle lovers of reason.

*Director*: How do you know they're not surrounded by those who appreciate gentle lovers of reason?

*Protégé*: Director.

*Director*: What? How do you know?

*Protégé*: They might be appreciated for being decent human beings. But it takes a gentle lover to know a gentle lover—and there aren't that many of them in the whole world; surely not enough to surround our friend.

*Director*: I'm not sure.

*Protégé*: Of what?

*Director*: How many gentle lovers of reason there actually are in the world.

*Protégé*: Most gentle lovers get crushed. So I think there aren't very many left.

*Director*: What happens to them when they're crushed? Are they dead?

*Protégé*: What would 'dead' mean?

*Director*: They lose all sight of reason.

*Protégé*: I think that happens.

*Director*: Maybe we need to change what we're saying.

*Protégé*: How so?

*Director*: Maybe we're not looking for gentle lovers. Maybe we're looking for vigorous lovers, the kind that won't get crushed.

*Protégé*: The kind that make their own luck?

*Director*: Sure. Why not?

*Protégé*: But reason speaks in a very soft voice. Vigorous lovers might not hear.

*Director*: Maybe that's why we have to amplify reason whenever we can.

*Protégé*: I don't like this very much.

*Director*: Why not?

*Protégé*: A soft word here differs in an important way from a loud word there.

*Director*: Yes, but what about our allies?

*Protégé*: What about them?

*Director*: We have to keep on winning them over. And good natured allies often want a loud word there.

*Protégé*: But it's not the same!

*Director*: Allies are never quite the same as friends. The question is—can we do without them?


~ ALLIES


*Protégé*: I thought the idea was to fight on our own.

*Director*: And so we must. But if we're trying to hold the line and we're vastly outnumbered?

*Protégé*: We stuff a few allies there?

*Director*: That doesn't do justice to who they are. The allies, too, want to fight.

*Protégé*: As a group?

*Director*: Yes.

*Protégé*: But we don't fight as a group. We fight alone as one. And the allies fight as one but never alone.

*Director*: Maybe they're smarter than us.

*Protégé*: I don't think so. They come to us for reason's commands.

*Director*: Does reason command?

*Protégé*: Reason suggests, then we command.

*Director*: Command our allies.

*Protégé*: Yes.

*Director*: But who put us in charge?

*Protégé*: They did.

*Director*: Why?

*Protégé*: They can sense we're in touch with the core.

*Director*: And that's why they allied with us?

*Protégé*: Yes, they know they deal with the core at a remove.

*Director*: And they want to be closer to the core.

*Protégé*: Well....

*Director*: Why the hesitation?

*Protégé*: If that's what they want, they would take steps.

*Director*: Is it better to deal with the core at a remove than not at all?

*Protégé*: Yes. Some reason is better than none.

*Director*: Are you sure?

*Protégé*: Aren't you?

*Director*: Sometimes I wonder. But let's say it's so. Still, I think we have to ask— what would happen with our allies if there were no enemies?

*Protégé*: There would be no need for them. And so I think we'd have to bring them in closer to the core.

*Director*: They would have to do that, want that on their own.

*Protégé*: And if they didn't?

*Director*: We might have found our new enemy.

## ~ Ways

*Director*: But enough of that. What are the ways of reason?

*Protégé*: Gentleness. And nothing more.

*Director*: Can the violent be gentle?

*Protégé*: That's a contradiction in terms.

*Director*: What if they're violent in some things but gentle in others?

*Protégé*: Then we have to be on guard.

*Director*: What if I'm violent toward the violent but gentle towards you? Should you be on guard?

*Protégé*: I suppose I should. What do you say to that?

*Director*: Good for you.

*Protégé*: I think we should always be on guard.

*Director*: At the risk of paranoia? That's a real risk, you know.

*Protégé*: When should we trust?

*Director*: When someone is gentle toward the gentle.

*Protégé*: That's all it takes?

*Director*: That's much, don't you think?

*Protégé*: I suppose it is. Especially when the gentle are on guard.

*Director*: Who likes to feel guarded against?

*Protégé*: You do, I think.

*Director*: It's true. I like to know my friends keep safe.

*Protégé*: You don't mind feeling shut out?

*Director*: Oh, they let me in soon enough.

*Protégé*: Why do they let you in?

*Director*: My ways are gentle and in touch with reason's core.

*Protégé*: I can understand why they'd let the gentle in. But how would they know you're in touch with reason's core?

*Director*: Because I seem weird, strange.

*Protégé*: That's reason not to let you in!

*Director*: To our enemies, yes. But to our friends? They'd let me in.

*Protégé*: Our friends trust the strange?

*Director*: The strange that tends towards reason, yes.

*Protégé*: And how do they know it tends that way?

*Director*: Because that's their tendency, too.

*Protégé*: It's as simple as that? We support whatever is in line with our tendencies?

*Director*: That's what our allies do.

*Protégé*: And what do we—we, *Director*—what do we do?

*Director*: Know the difference between allies and friends.

*Protégé*: What is that difference?

*Director*: Mostly? We're with our allies in the fight. But our friends are with us in peace.

*Protégé*: But you're someone who's always in the fight!

*Director*: Are we in the fight now?

*Protégé*: I can't tell.

*Director*: Can you tell if you're an ally or a friend?

*Protégé*: I honestly can't.

*Director*: Then maybe you're both. Is that so bad? Or would you rather be a friend and no ally here?

*Protégé*: No, I'd rather be both.

*Director*: And if you were forced to choose?

*Protégé*: Forced? I'd say violence is being done.


~ Choice


*Director*: The violent force us to choose?

*Protégé*: I think they do. Don't you?

*Director*: Any time someone forces us to do something—choose, whatever—I'd say violence is in play.

*Protégé*: But there are times when we have to choose, no force from others—choose of necessity. Is necessity violent with us?

*Director*: Necessity can be harsh, can be violent with us, yes. It can be very hard to obey.

*Protégé*: And if we don't?

*Director*: We pay the price.

*Protégé*: But you say it 'can be' hard to obey. Are there times when it's easy?

*Director*: Certainly. And then necessity is sweet.

*Protégé*: But not everyone knows this. They think necessity is always bitter.

*Director*: I'm very sorry for them. So maybe this is part of my fight.

*Protégé*: To prove necessity can be sweet?

*Director*: Why not? We should all try to stay on its good side, if we can.

*Protégé*: But this begs a question. How do we know something is necessary? What if the coward in us says, 'Run away—because it's necessary to run away'? But, really, it's not necessary. It's just the coward's way.

*Director*: Only the inwardly honest can know necessity for what it is.

*Protégé*: I like what that means.

*Director*: What does it mean?

*Protégé*: That necessity is in touch with reason's core.

*Director*: That's the only place we'll find true necessity.

*Protégé*: Every time we look?

*Director*: If we open our eyes, we'll see.

*Protégé*: But what if we're afraid? Necessity can be a terrible thing, you know—well beyond bitter.

*Director*: And when we're in the habit of following it, no matter what, it grows sweet.

*Protégé*: I thought it was sweet when it's easy.

*Director*: There's a sweetness in well-done hard things, too. But the point is that we must embrace necessity all the way to the bottom of our heart. Then, and only then, do things go well.

*Protégé*: Tell me something, *Director*. Can we be honest when it comes to reason and necessity but be dishonest with all the rest?

*Director*: Is 'all the rest' violence?

*Protégé*: Yes, let's say it is.

*Director*: What do you think?

*Protégé*: I don't think we can.

*Director*: Why not?

*Protégé*: Because we said things are fluid.

*Director*: Yes, we did. But we should note—they're not as fluid as they might seem. But why do you bring this up?

*Protégé*: Because if things are fluid, people can change—and we shouldn't lie to those who can change.

*Director*: Change for the better.

*Protégé*: Of course.

*Director*: Then we lie only of necessity.

*Protégé*: And the rest of the time we speak the always and forever truth.


~ Forever


*Director*: That, my friend, is where we differ.

*Protégé*: Why?

*Director*: Because that's what the violent think about truth.

*Protégé*: What are you talking about?

*Director*: The violent aren't open to the evolution of truth.

*Protégé*: The violent aren't open to lies?

*Director*: It's not a lie to change your mind in accordance with developments. And if a truth you spoke under prior circumstances ties you up, more fool you. Truth will evolve as you provide therapy, *Protégé*. And you will make mistakes.

*Protégé*: Until I get my mind in tune with developments?

*Director*: Yes. And you may have to go back on things you said. Will you feel bad about that?

*Protégé*: I hope not.

*Director*: Learn from your mistakes, and then forget them.

*Protégé*: But if we forget the mistakes maybe we'll forget what we learned.

*Director*: I don't see how. Mistakes take us down a certain path. On this path, we have to find truth. That's the whole point, to find that truth. And when we have, we must go forward with truth, not back.

*Protégé*: So we can safely forget the 'back', the mistakes.

*Director*: Yes. And I recommend it.

*Protégé*: Why?

*Director*: Less baggage to carry with us. Emotional baggage, intellectual baggage—you name it.

*Protégé*: But let's get back to the point. You really don't think truth is forever?

*Director*: Even the core of reason might not be forever.

*Protégé*: So what are you saying? Reason itself is only good enough for now?

*Director*: It's better than 'good enough', of course. But is it forever? I really don't know. But that makes our dedication to it all the more... touching.

*Protégé*: You'd better explain.

*Director*: How praiseworthy is it to support something that is no doubt the eternal best thing? But if there are doubts? If we're not sure reason is forever? There's something poignant in standing up for this. Do you see what I mean?

*Protégé*: I think I do. There's something human in this.

*Director*: Yes, precisely. And the violent force the human into inhuman certainty.

*Protégé*: They make it into something other than it is.

*Director*: Right. But we, we don't do violence to the facts. We let them speak for themselves, unsettling as they might be.

*Protégé*: As weird, strange, or uncanny as they might be. But I still think we can't change our minds suddenly without causing harm.

*Director*: Harm to ourselves?

*Protégé*: Sure, and harm to others.

*Director*: What others?

*Protégé*: The people who depend on us, on what we think.

*Director*: Why do they depend?

*Protégé*: They want to know.

*Director*: And they know by leaning on what we think?

*Protégé*: Often times? Yes.

*Director*: I can hardly believe I'm hearing this from you. Protégé, we need to know on our own, regardless of what others think.

*Protégé*: Yes, but not everyone can go to the core.

*Director*: Ah, so you think there's a fundamental difference between people.

*Protégé*: I'm not sure I'm saying that. Sometimes circumstances get in the way.

*Director*: Circumstances always get in the way. The difference is in who dares to go beyond them.


~ Unease


*Protégé*: But you're saying we're all the same in that we all have a choice.

*Director*: No, I'm saying some of us have it in us; others don't.

*Protégé*: So people can't change?

*Director*: They can learn more about what they are. And this is a change, a very real and important change. But not all can come to thrive with the core in the same way possible for you.

*Protégé*: Okay. So if people can't thrive that way, is there any point in speaking gentle reason to the violent?

*Director*: Others might be present and learn from what we speak. And if the situation is more fluid than we think, maybe we'll see some change in the violent, too.

*Protégé*: But what if the situation is much more fluid than we think? What if it's simply fluid?

*Director*: Then we wouldn't be speaking to the violent. They wouldn't be part of that situation.

*Protégé*: Why not?

*Director*: The violent just aren't that fluid. It would take us some time to explain why this is so.

*Protégé*: No, that's fine. I just want to know—who is that fluid?

*Director*: Reasoned friends. But we can, of course, be wrong about certain individuals. Wrong about their fluidity; wrong about whether they truly are friends.

*Protégé*: That's what I was wondering.

*Director*: Wonder is part of the strangeness of reason. That's why you feel unease. Reason doesn't work like a textbook might make you think.

*Protégé*: What is reason?

*Director*: Life. Life is full of uncertainty, and contradiction, and things that make us afraid. We have to learn to live with this, and hold on tight to reason whenever we can.

*Protégé*: But didn't you say something about holding on loosely?

*Director*: I was talking about something else. We should hold on tight to reason whenever we can. I stand by this, *Protégé*.

*Protégé*: For now?

*Director*: Of course for now. When else would I stand by it? Then? I think you're going to learn a lot about these things once you're in business as a therapist. People will ask you what you're asking me.

*Protégé*: Do you see that as justice?

*Director*: No, I don't. I see it as somewhat comical, I have to admit. But now I realize I shouldn't have said that. It can't seem funny to you now.

*Protégé*: You said you have to admit it, as if necessity were forcing your hand. But then you say you shouldn't have said it at all. So what's going on here, *Director*?

*Director*: You have me at a loss. I need to retreat to the core.

*Protégé*: And now you're saying I'm growing violent with you? Why else would you have to retreat?

*Director*: Protégé, sometimes this is what happens when people of reason converse. It's one of the reasons I say we need to fight alone.

*Protégé*: What are you saying happens?

*Director*: Misunderstanding and... worse.

*Protégé*: Violence?

*Director*: Yes, on both parts.

*Protégé*: Have you been violent with me today?

*Director*: I made some abrupt transitions. Abruptness and violence often go hand in hand.

*Protégé*: When is abruptness not violent?

*Director*: When it saves your life.

*Protégé*: What do you mean?

*Director*: Sometimes the violent want to suffocate you. An abrupt departure can save your life.

*Protégé*: That makes sense. I've experienced this first hand. But I still felt bad about the departures.

*Director*: Well, you shouldn't. The violent certainly didn't feel bad about smothering you. Why should you feel bad about saving your life?

*Protégé*: The violent are tricky. They sometimes use manners to their advantage.

*Director*: Yes, they want to control you with manners. They want you to be predictable, mannered, so they can work their harm.

*Protégé*: But to be sure, we're not saying manners are bad.

*Director*: No, certainly not. Manners often allow reason to speak.

*Protégé*: It's like this with everything, isn't it?

*Director*: What do you mean?

*Protégé*: Everything—and I mean everything—can be used for good or ill.

*Director*: Yes. Does that make you uneasy?

*Protégé*: It makes me scared.


~ SCARED


*Director*: Maybe it's better to be scared than uneasy.

*Protégé*: Why would you say that?

*Director*: Fear is definite; unease is vague.

*Protégé*: I'm not sure the two are quite that distinct.

*Director*: Then let's drive our unease into solid fear, and confront that fear. What do you think about that?

*Protégé*: We should always choose the definite over the vague?

*Director*: When reasoning? Yes.

*Protégé*: And you're always reasoning.

*Director*: Unless I'm asleep. How about you?

*Protégé*: I do less reasoning than running from my vague fears.

*Director*: And when you run from your vague fears?

*Protégé*: I wish I hadn't run. So what should I do?

*Director*: Reason your way out of the mess.

*Protégé*: Is that more important than facing my fears?

*Director*: You don't really know what your fears are. Reason, and come to knowledge of what they are, as soon as you can.

*Protégé*: And if I don't?

*Director*: The vagueness you feel about them can lead to an existential crisis.

*Protégé*: Unlike fears that are known?

*Director*: Well, chronic fear, known fear, can lead to crisis, too.

*Protégé*: Even if we stand our ground?

*Director*: Sometimes.

*Protégé*: So there are times when we should run?

*Director*: When the ground is bad? It might be time to retreat. Only you would know. But you can't know if you don't have a grip on your fear.

*Protégé*: You mean we have to understand the fear.

*Director*: Yes.

*Protégé*: I think you're right. I'd rather be out-and-out afraid of something than have some vague, unknowing sense of unease. There's something more honest in that.

*Director*: Vagueness haunts like no fear can.

*Protégé*: The vague makes life seem gray.

*Director*: You must, must, bring color to your life—even if it's the color of fear.

*Protégé*: I see color here with you now.

*Director*: Good. But I'll tell you something. When I'm leaving the core, I sometimes feel unease.

*Protégé*: Because your world turns upside down?

*Director*: Yes. Or the ground opens up at my feet. Anyway, when I feel this unease I have to think my way through, back to the colors of light.

*Protégé*: But isn't there color at the core? Why not go back?

*Director*: Because the core is demanding and we grow tired.

*Protégé*: It's really that simple?

*Director*: It really is.

*Protégé*: In what sense is the core demanding?

*Director*: The core is manifold and places demands on us from every side.

*Protégé*: What kinds of demands?

*Director*: It varies from person to person.

*Protégé*: I think I know less about the core now than I did before.

*Director*: Sorry. I can only tell you what I've seen. But maybe this is a sign.

*Protégé*: What kind of sign?

*Director*: I'm always tempted to make points that invite my friends to go straight to the core.

*Protégé*: And the sign tells you that we should take a more roundabout way?

*Director*: Yes, a way that prepares us so we're not overwhelmed.

*Protégé*: And what about on our way back from the core?

*Director*: That's often an abrupt transition.

*Protégé*: What can we do to mitigate the abruptness, the shock to our system?

*Director*: Work.

*Protégé*: What do you mean?

*Director*: It takes work to ease our way back from the core. We have to take it a careful step at a time. We have to adjust to what we've learned. And I have to warn you—it's exhausting.

*Protégé*: I'm not afraid of work.

*Director*: I noticed. We've been doing some work today.

*Protégé*: Our conversation?

*Director*: Our dialogue, yes. Dialogue gives us something to think about and remember. It leads us to the core without taking us all the way. We can only go all the way on our own.

*Protégé*: So we haven't been to the core today.

*Director*: No, we haven't. But we have said many things that can help us on our way there.

*Protégé*: And that's good enough?

*Director*: Good enough? No, it's great.


~ Good, Again


*Protégé*: Does only good come of the core?

*Director*: It depends what we mean by good.

*Protégé*: What might we mean?

*Director*: Good or 'good'. 'Good' never comes of the core.

*Protégé*: Let me ask you this. Do the violent have good in their lives?

*Director*: No.

*Protégé:* They have 'good'?

*Director:* Yes.

*Protégé:* If the violent dominate the world, does that mean 'good' dominates the world?

*Director:* Yes.

*Protégé:* Does good seem bad to those taken up with 'good'?

*Director:* You know it does.

*Protégé:* So our trips to the core are suspect at best.

*Director:* In such a world? Correct.

*Protégé:* We have to win the battle, the battle for good.

*Director:* Good, goodness, the good—whatever you want to call it.

*Protégé:* Why can't the violent know the good?

*Director:* Because the good derives from the core. Anything that derives from the core is touched with reason. The violent hate reason, reason in its whole. So do you see why the violent can't know the good?

*Protégé:* They can't know the good because their hate gets in the way.

*Director:* Yes.

*Protégé:* What if they get rid of their hate?

*Director:* Are you asking what happens if they change their nature?

*Protégé:* I guess I am. But it occurs to me—does this mean we, the good, know no hate?

*Director:* I prefer to say we who know the good, as opposed to we who are the good. But I take your point. Can we hate? Yes. Do we hate? Sometimes. What happens when we hate? We might lose touch with the core.

*Protégé:* But you don't know?

*Director:* There might be reason to hate. I don't know. When I feel hate, I turn to the core and it fades away. But maybe another could hold on to reasoned hate while in touch with the core. It sounds bad to say. But I really don't know.

*Protégé:* I think we need to know.

*Director:* Do you have hate you want to hold on to?

*Protégé:* I hate the violent. How can you fight them without hating them, *Director*?

*Director:* I don't know. I just fight. I know there's a reason to fight. That's enough for me. Besides, hate might cloud my judgment.

*Protégé*: That's a good point. I hadn't thought of that.

*Director*: I recommend that when you're a therapist you should steer well clear of hate.

*Protégé*: Well, in that context of course.

*Director*: Yes, but people will come to you damaged by the violent. You might love these people. Might you not hate those who did this to them?

*Protégé*: You're right. I think I would.

*Director*: Would you teach your clients your hate?

*Protégé*: No, that doesn't seem right. But won't they already have hatred in them?

*Director*: Some will, I'd guess. What will you do with them? Nurture the hate?

*Protégé*: I don't think that's a good idea.

*Director*: Why not?

*Protégé*: Hate won't help you heal.

*Director*: So you'll tell them to save the hatred for when they're better?

*Protégé*: You want me to teach against hate.

*Director*: I want you to do what's in your heart. You don't strike me as a great hater. Yes, I think you have some hate. But that's not how you'll steer your life.

*Protégé*: How do you know?

*Director*: I know who you are.


## ~ READY


*Protégé*: I wish I could say I know myself as well as you seem to know me!

*Director*: You just might not be ready.

*Protégé*: We have to be ready to know ourselves?

*Director*: Oh, yes. Certainly.

*Protégé*: Do you know yourself?

*Director*: Mostly, I think.

*Protégé*: When did you learn what you are?

*Director*: I'd rather not say.

*Protégé*: But you can trace it to a specific time and place?

*Director*: I can. But I might be mistaken in this. I live every day questioning whether I'm wrong, whether I really know.

*Protégé*: But isn't that a waste of energy?

*Director*: No, I draw energy from the questioning.

*Protégé*: Somehow I don't believe you.

*Director*: A sign that you're not ready.

*Protégé*: Look, I believe questioning others can energize you. But to question yourself?

*Director*: Question yourself as though you were another. There's your energy, friend.

*Protégé*: It doesn't work that way.

*Director*: Have you tried?

*Protégé*: No.

*Director*: Then how can you say? Right now you just believe it doesn't work that way. You don't actually know.

*Protégé*: Well, it's true. Sometimes we think we know when we don't.

*Director*: And that's what friends are for. They help each other know. They clear up mistaken beliefs.

*Protégé*: So you admit you might not know yourself and only believe you do?

*Director*: No doubt. And if I only believe, I surely want to know. So when you're ready, help me if you can.

*Protégé*: If I can? Why wouldn't I be able to help?

*Director*: I might grow violent with you.

*Protégé*: I don't think you would. It's not in your nature.

*Director*: Yes, but we can act against our natures when under the proper stress.

~ STRESS

*Protégé*: You make me wonder. What if the world is in such a state that all of the gentle are under just the right stress?

*Director*: That's a very important question.

*Protégé*: Do you think it's possible?

*Director*: I do. In fact, that's my greatest fear.

*Protégé*: Why is that your greatest fear?

*Director*: Because it would cause us to lose touch with the core, and we might never find it again.

*Protégé*: Then violence would be all.

*Director*: And we wouldn't even know that's what it is.

*Protégé*: We wouldn't know violence is violence?

*Director*: There would be nothing to compare it to. It would seem to us that that's just how the world is, how it works. And, yes, we'd feel strange. But we'd simply think something is wrong with us. At best we'd be in a quandary all our lives.

*Protégé*: How do we prevent this?

*Director*: We do whatever it takes not to let the stress get to us.

*Protégé*: And you really mean whatever.

*Director*: Yes.

*Protégé*: What about others? Can we help them with their stress?

*Director*: We can be an example to them. And yes, we can point some things out to them about themselves. But they have to do the heavy lifting.

*Protégé*: I know a way to help relieve some stress.

*Director*: What way? I could use a little relief myself.

*Protégé*: You can play with my kittens.

*Director*: Yes! That is true stress relief. Can you see why the kittens are important?

*Protégé*: I can. They are as important as your battles.

*Director*: Exactly. You don't know how glad I am you see this now.

*Protégé*: The kittens are my therapy animals. I'll let all my clients play with them, too—especially those returning from the front.

*Director*: Each of the gentle are at the front every single day.

*Protégé*: Maybe that's my mission in life. I'll find as many kittens as I can and give them to reason's soldiers.

*Director*: Tell me now. What is a kitten?

*Protégé*: Something that makes you feel good about yourself. It can't be helped. You see the kitten play and you cannot help but smile.

*Director*: If you're a gentle soul, you mean.

*Protégé*: Yes, of course. But there's something more.

*Director*: What more?

*Protégé*: The kitten brings you love.

*Director*: Ah, something a battle-scarred veteran truly needs.

*Protégé*: Love will heal your wounds and ready you for another fight. It all works out.

*Director*: But these special kittens, do they reason with us?

*Protégé*: Of course they do!

*Director*: And you're saying those who reason can play?

*Protégé*: I am. And it's a wonderful thing.

## ~ Play

*Protégé*: The violent hate it when we play.

*Director*: Why?

*Protégé*: It shows that we're not intimidated by them.

*Director*: And they grow mad?

*Protégé*: Of course.

*Director*: I like it when they grow mad.

*Protégé*: How come?

*Director*: They make mistakes. And when they make enough mistakes, they lose the fight.

*Protégé*: Then we should play more often.

*Director*: I think that's a good idea. But really, what does it mean to play with reason?

*Protégé*: Haven't you ever heard a gentle comedian?

*Director*: Tell me what they do.

*Protégé*: Gentle comedians joke about the enemy.

*Director*: In ear shot of the enemy?

*Protégé*: Yes, they're not afraid.

*Director*: And they tell the truth?

*Protégé*: And they reason about the truth. And their reasons are very funny.

*Director*: The violent must hate this sort of thing.

*Protégé*: Of course they do. They want to censor the comedians.

*Director*: On what grounds?

*Protégé*: Insensitivity.

*Director*: That's a good one.

*Protégé*: It is. These comedians are very sensitive.

*Director*: I'm sure they are. And their work is very important. It might serve to separate the gentle from the violent.

*Protégé*: What do you mean?

*Director*: The gentle are born to the violent all the time. It takes great effort to separate them. These comedians might help by making the gentle laugh when none of those around them are laughing.

*Protégé*: Won't that set the gentle up for trouble?

*Director*: These gentle were set up for trouble from the day they were born. Laughter that makes you see you're different is a gentle way of prodding you to take certain steps.

*Protégé*: What kind of steps?

*Director*: For one, they might hang around after the show and meet the comedian. It's very important that these comedians be open to conversation with anyone from the audience who wants to talk.

*Protégé*: Even the violent?

*Director*: Even so. Better a thousand dreadful conversations and one true connection than no connection at all.

*Protégé*: I completely agree. But with all these dreadful conversations, how do they keep their sense of humor intact?

*Director*: Through hope. Hope that they'll connect. And when they do, oh how the humor roars!


~ HUMOR


*Protégé*: They might scare the gentle off!

*Director*: No, because it's the gentle who roar, roar in laughter like they've never before.

*Protégé*: I want laughter like that.

*Director*: Connect with a gentle comedian, then. But tell me something, *Protégé*. How do these comedians develop their humor?

*Protégé*: Through resistance to their violent surroundings.

*Director*: Yes, I think that's true. Their gentle humor stands out against a backdrop of violence. Take the violence away and it's not so funny anymore.

*Protégé*: So you're telling me there are gentle ones who need the violent in order to be what they are?

*Director*: Well, I'd rather put it like this. Fun at the expense of the violent is their fight. And we all need our fight.

*Protégé*: But won't the violent try to shut the comedians up?

*Director*: That's part of the fight.

*Protégé*: That puts these gentle ones at risk.

*Director*: We're all at risk in this world.

*Protégé*: If I'm a therapist, how am I at risk?

*Director*: Do you think your patients will all be singing sweet reason's tune?

*Protégé*: Of course not. That's why they'll come to me.

*Director*: They struggle with violence within. Well, what if the violence wins out?

*Protégé*: Then I'm at risk.

*Director*: Yes. But maybe not in the way you might think. They're not going to lunge at you from across the room.

*Protégé*: What will they do?

*Director*: Slowly poison your mind.

*Protégé*: What's the antidote to this?

*Director*: Comedy. Very good laughs.

*Protégé*: And if I can't laugh?

*Director*: Then damage has been done.


~ PHILOSOPHY


*Protégé*: Is philosophy ever funny?

*Director*: Typically not the philosophy itself, but its after effects can be.

*Protégé*: How so?

*Director*: Sometimes when the violent encounter philosophy, they find themselves perplexed.

*Protégé*: They don't know what to make of philosophy.

*Director*: Right. And their struggle to make sense of it is comical to those who know what philosophy is.

*Protégé*: But why not try to help them understand?

*Director*: Who, the violent? Are we back at this again?

*Protégé*: No, I take the point. Only the gentle can understand. And it's good the violent are perplexed. Instead of using their energy to attack the gentle, they get caught in philosophy's web. What draws them in?

*Director*: Suspicion.

*Protégé*: What do they suspect?

*Director*: That where there's smoke there must be fire.

*Protégé*: They want to catch philosophy up.

*Director*: Yes. They want a reason to condemn philosophy.

*Protégé*: But there is no reason, is there.

*Director*: There's nothing but words.

*Protégé*: Yes, but the violent know they, the violent, can do harm with their words, harm to the gentle. They must believe the gentle can somehow use words to harm them.

*Director*: And there's the comedy. They approach our words—in books, in plays, in person—as though they might have terrible power.

*Protégé*: But they do have power—with the gentle at heart.

*Director*: Yes, but the violent are far from gentle at heart. So the words, intended for like others, have no effect on them.

*Protégé*: But this lack of effect must drive them insane!

*Director*: Can you give an example?

*Protégé*: I spent a whole summer reading Plato's works. My violent classmates made fun of me, of course. They couldn't see what there was to it that I would be so engrossed. One of them got a copy of the book and read. And he read and he read, growing outraged as he did.

*Director*: He didn't like what he read?

*Protégé*: He couldn't see the point.

*Director*: So what did he conclude?

*Protégé*: That I and others like me were crazy, *Director*. Fools. But he had this nagging doubt.

*Director*: What doubt?

*Protégé*: That it was he who was somehow the fool.

*Director*: Why do you think he had this doubt?

*Protégé*: He and I were tied for top of the class. He knew I had a keen mind. And it bothered him that he just couldn't understand why I cared about these ancient works.

*Director*: Hmm.

*Protégé*: What is it?

*Director*: Sometimes the ancient exercises a powerful effect on the violent mind.

*Protégé*: Why do you think that is?

*Director*: The violent like to lose themselves in the past. They laze about and swat the occasional reasoned fly.

*Protégé*: Why do some laze like this and others grow angry?

*Director*: I don't know. But I do know the angry also swat reasoned flies.

*Protégé*: Are you suggesting I'm a fly?

*Director*: You're no fly. You're a fierce cat. Reason's cat.

*Protégé*: I'd like to think that's true.

*Director*: But it is true. You're a fierce cat with kittens at home.

*Protégé*: I'll protect them with my life.

*Director*: Good. Because it might come to that one day.


~ RISK


*Protégé*: In my practice of therapy?

*Director*: What do you think happens if one of your clients is terribly abused by a reasonless spouse?

*Protégé*: I'd encourage them to leave and start fresh on their own.

*Director*: So they leave. And the spouse puts two and two together and realizes you're the one.

*Protégé*: The one who what?

*Director*: Seduced the spouse away. Might your life not be at risk?

*Protégé*: Therapists deal with powerful things. My life might be at risk.

*Director*: Would you back down because of the risk? Would you refuse to tell your client what they need to hear?

*Protégé*: What would I be if I did?

*Director*: So you'd accept the risk?

*Protégé*: For the sake of all the meaning in my life, I would.

*Director*: If someone were to threaten you for this, what would you do?

*Protégé*: I'd call you.

*Director*: And what would I do?

*Protégé*: Fight fire with fire.

*Director*: You couldn't do that?

*Protégé*: My metaphor is kittens. Yours is the fight.

*Director*: Fair enough.

*Protégé*: So would you bring the fight?

*Director*: With pleasure.

*Protégé*: And that's reason enough for me to bring the fight to you!

*Director*: Is pleasure always 'reason enough'?

*Protégé*: Well, I have to wonder about the violent and their pleasures.

*Director*: I don't think they have true pleasure.

*Protégé*: Not even when they're harming us?

*Director*: They only have pleasure then if we let them.

*Protégé*: They only have pleasure if we let them see we're hurt?

*Director*: Yes. So, Protégé, never let them see that it hurts.

*Protégé*: Never?

*Director*: Never, unto death.

*Protégé*: That's a very serious thing.

*Director*: What, death? How do we know if it is or it isn't?

*Protégé*: It's... death!

*Director*: So what?

*Protégé*: Are you really that brave?

*Director*: We're only brave when we face things we know are bad. I've never experienced death. Have you?

*Protégé*: Of course not.

*Director*: Then how do we know it's bad?

*Protégé*: You're really asking me why death is bad?

*Director*: I am. Why?

*Protégé*: Because!

*Director*: Well, when we reduce it to 'why' and 'because', there's not much more to say. But I will say this. To answer 'why' with nothing more than 'because' is a violent sort of thing.

*Protégé*: Why?

*Director*: Because we have to assume that 'why' just might want to know.


### ~ Why


*Protégé*: Why do we have to make that assumption? So many are violent in this world. They ask why. But do they really want to know?

*Director*: It's true. Not many of them do.

*Protégé*: Then why do we assume they really want to know?

*Director*: Because we might be wrong, and they might. What harm does it do to assume they might?

*Protégé*: It might do harm to us!

*Director*: Because we offer our reasons up for all to see? No, no harm will come of that—provided our reasons are good.

*Protégé*: Well, that's the thing. Our reasons are good, not 'good'. That's why they'll do us harm.

*Director*: So we should hide? And take our good reasons with us?

*Protégé*: Well, I'm not saying we should hide.

*Director*: Then what are you saying?

*Protégé*: We need to be careful here, that's all.

*Director*: Careful to share only with those who deserve it?

*Protégé*: Yes.

*Director*: How can we know they deserve it?

*Protégé*: We share a thing or two and see how they react.

*Director*: How should they react?

*Protégé*: They'll share some things with us.

*Director*: Reciprocation is the key?

*Protégé*: Don't you think it should be?

*Director*: You have a point. But what if they don't have much to reciprocate with?

*Protégé*: What do you mean?

*Director*: What if they are a gentle nature born into a violent world? They've spent their life so far just trying to exist. What would they have to share?

*Protégé*: Stories from the front.

*Director*: But they're not stories to them. They're more than stories. They're something very personal and real.

*Protégé*: *Director*, when we meet someone we sense will understand, and haven't had someone like that before—we share.

*Director*: Do we? What if we're afraid?

*Protégé*: Then that's very sad.

*Director*: I say we don't worry too much about reciprocation. We take our time. We share some things. But we don't overwhelm.

*Protégé*: Overwhelming is a novice mistake?

*Director*: Yes. Experience teaches us patience.

*Protégé*: But what if there's no time?

*Director*: There's really no time? Then we're direct.

*Protégé*: How?

*Director*: We tell them the ones around them, the violent ones—they are, at best, dead.

*Protégé*: And what, we just leave them with that?

*Director*: We hope one day they'll understand. After all, how could they forget?

*Protégé*: No one forgets something like that. Especially when it rings true.


### ～ Violence, Yet Again


*Protégé*: But remind me why it's true.

*Director*: Because the violent are never in touch with reason's core.

*Protégé*: And without reason we're nothing more than violent beasts.

*Director*: That doesn't do justice to the beasts.

*Protégé*: But you know what I mean.

*Director*: I do. And yes, gentle reason is the very thin line. On one side we're humans; on the other we're... beasts.

*Protégé*: Why is the line thin?

*Director*: Because it's very easy to cross. Do you think because we're once with reason we're always with reason?

*Protégé*: No. But then what are we?

*Director*: What we are is capable of crossing the line and getting into very big trouble. Even in this trouble we are what we are. But we're in trouble nonetheless.

*Protégé*: Are the violent at heart capable of crossing the line into our side of things?

*Director*: It happens from time to time. But they feel hopelessly lost and crash around like a bull in a china shop.

*Protégé*: Is gentle reason really as delicate as china?

*Director*: Some reason is very tough and can withstand the bulls. Other reason is fragile, yes.

*Protégé*: So tough reason should guard the border.

*Director*: And it does. But sometimes it sleeps and the bulls get in.

*Protégé*: I didn't think reason would sleep.

*Director*: Remember, reason itself is in the core. It's the people of reason, tough reason, who sometimes sleep.

*Protégé*: Do the people of delicate reason sleep?

*Director*: All people sleep, my friend.

*Protégé*: Then we need more on the border.

*Director*: More on the front, yes.

*Protégé*: There's a constant battle on the border, isn't there?

*Director*: Yes, there is.

*Protégé*: Can we ever win?

*Director*: What, you mean kill all the bad? I don't know. From what I've seen it seems very unlikely. And then there's the fear.

*Protégé*: What fear?

*Director*: Do you remember my fear about just the right stress making us lose touch with reason?

*Protégé*: Yes, what of it?

*Director*: I have a fear that the loss of friction with the enemy might make us lose touch with the core.

*Protégé*: Why would it do that? What good is friction?

*Director*: Friction makes us think. Without friction we might be like so many plants.

*Protégé*: Vegetables?

*Director*: Vegetables, sure. What do you think?

*Protégé*: I don't know. You might be right. How would we know short of total victory?

*Director*: Isolated victories might give us the sense. Suppose we clear the enemy from our sector. We should sit back and see how we feel.

*Protégé*: See if we feel like reasoning.

*Director*: Yes. And I don't mean right away. We need to give it time.

*Protégé*: Of course. In the wash of emotions from victory we might not reason at all. But how much time?

*Director*: I don't know. Maybe a day?

*Protégé*: A day? I was thinking more like several months!

*Director*: Okay, but I'm not sure the violent would fail to reinforce the front for that long.

*Protégé*: Why do they even care?

*Director*: What do you mean?

*Protégé*: About the front, about us.


~ Us


*Director*: The violent prey on the meek.

*Protégé*: We're gentle, not meek. And we're strong. Why are you smiling?

*Director*: Because you're showing your strength. That makes me smile.

*Protégé*: Why?

*Director*: Because it hints at victory. Victories make me smile.

*Protégé*: That's the point, isn't it? Not one great big victory, but many little victories along the way.

*Director*: Some medium sized ones, too.

*Protégé*: Oh, stop kidding. I'm being serious.

*Director*: So am I. Yes, it's mostly small victories. But sometimes we win over some friends.

*Protégé*: You mean we help some see what they are.

*Director*: Yes. And that brings them to us.

*Protégé*: What if they don't want to be part of us?

*Director*: That happens from time to time. They go undercover among the enemy.

*Protégé*: But they still serve the cause?

*Director*: In their way, yes. I catch sight of them now and then.

*Protégé*: How do you know where to look?

*Director*: There's an explosion among the violent. You can't fail to see it.

*Protégé*: What, it's all over the media?

*Director*: It's usually just word of mouth—aftershocks, ripples of sorts.

*Protégé*: The undercover one caused the explosion? How?

*Director*: By setting things up in just the right way.

*Protégé*: I don't understand.

*Director*: Reason puts unreason on a collision course.

*Protégé*: And the collision is the explosion?

*Director*: Yes.

*Protégé*: And what happens with the violent then?

*Director*: Some of them grow afraid and retreat into a shell.

*Protégé*: And the rest?

*Director*: They redouble their attacks all along the line.

*Protégé*: But then is it worth it?

*Director*: Is what worth it?

*Protégé*: The actions of the undercover us!

*Director*: I think so. If you could only see the look on those violent faces. It's worth it.

*Protégé*: After this happens, do they come back to us?

*Director*: The undercover? They never left us, friend.

*Protégé*: But they're all alone.

*Director*: In one sense, yes. In another, they couldn't be less alone. They're with us all.

*Protégé*: They're with me?

*Director*: In ways you don't yet know.

*Protégé*: I want to know all about us.

*Director*: Well, start with me. I'm with us.

*Protégé*: Can you introduce me to others?

*Director*: I can. Let's see if your potential friend is one.

*Protégé*: I hope so. But if he's not, that's okay.

*Director*: Really?

*Protégé*: Really. There are a couple of other interesting people in my class.

*Director*: So there's even more reason for me to register for a course?

*Protégé*: There is. Greek verbs always come in handy.


~ Utility, Skepsis


*Director*: Tell me something, *Protégé*. Are you more of a utilitarian or are you a skeptic?

*Protégé*: I didn't know those two were mutually exclusive.

*Director*: Ah, you're encouraging me.

*Protégé*: Why, what are you?

*Director*: I'm someone who thinks there can be utility to skepticism.

*Protégé*: But you're not a skeptic?

*Director*: No, I'm not. There are some things I know are true, let the skeptics assault them as they will.

*Protégé*: Are you suggesting skeptics, philosophical skeptics, can be violent?

*Director*: Oh, yes. They certainly can. They do violence to reason out of principle.

*Protégé*: The principle of doubt?

*Director*: Yes.

*Protégé*: But isn't doubt part of reason?

*Director*: Part, not whole. It's easy to doubt when you doubt everything, every single thing, on principle.

*Protégé*: What can be done about them?

*Director*: We have to treat them as the enemy they are.

*Protégé*: But I don't like to think of philosophers as enemies.

*Director*: They're 'philosophers', my friend. The violent undercover. And I'd like to give them something to believe.

*Protégé*: A belief that would hurt them?

*Director*: A belief that would kill them, *Protégé*.

*Protégé*: I still don't like the idea of killing philosophers.

*Director*: 'Philosophers'.

*Protégé*: Even so.

*Director*: You still think the enemy is only an enemy because of some misunderstanding, don't you?

*Protégé*: Maybe I do.

*Director*: Tell me. What does eternal comprehensive doubt do to someone who is struggling to see the good in themselves?

*Protégé*: It makes it harder for them to see.

*Director*: And we, you and I, we want them to see. See the good.

*Protégé*: Yes.

*Director*: And we know what's good.

*Protégé*: Well....

*Director*: Well what?

*Protégé*: The question of the good is as old as all philosophy.

*Director*: No it's not. The earliest philosophers knew the good. It was Plato's big talk about the good that started the trouble.

*Protégé*: Didn't Socrates start the trouble?

*Director*: Sure. But in the end, what's the difference?

*Protégé*: What do you mean?

*Director*: We don't know what Socrates said. We know what Plato said.

*Protégé*: But Plato said what Socrates said.

*Director*: Did he?

*Protégé*: You... have a point.

*Director*: I'm not the first to make it. But it bears repeating.

*Protégé*: How do I know you're not a philosophical skeptic attacking the philosophical tradition on principle?

*Director*: Because there's utility in my attack.

*Protégé*: What utility?

*Director*: It's useful to break the surface of crusty tradition in order to get to the liquor beneath.

*Protégé*: And you don't mean alcoholic liquor.

*Director*: No, I don't. I mean the alternate meaning of that word. And that purpose of mine—to get beneath the crust—shows I'm not some scarecrow of a philosopher attacking on principle.

*Protégé*: I've never heard you speak like this.

*Director*: I'm speaking with force because there's a danger for us here.

*Protégé*: For you and me?

*Director*: For all of us, friend.


## ~ DANGER

*Protégé*: What's the danger?

*Director*: Philosophy has been compromised. We can no longer speak of philosophy simply as some good thing. We have to put philosophy to the test.

*Protégé*: When did this compromise happen?

*Director*: As soon as philosophy was born.

*Protégé*: Director.

*Director*: What? It's true!

*Protégé*: I don't doubt it. So what will you do? Go around testing every so-called philosopher?

*Director*: Yes.

*Protégé*: That's a hopeless struggle.

*Director*: Why?

*Protégé*: Because for every 'philosopher' you put down a thousand more are born.

*Director*: Yes, it's quite the battle. That's why I want to be like the three-hundred Spartans who held the Persians off at the pass.

*Protégé*: Just long enough for someone like me to get away?

*Director*: Yes. But don't worry. I'll get away, too. And take my position again on the line.

*Protégé*: There must be a better metaphor.

*Director*: What do you mean?

*Protégé*: It's not all killing and battles and such. That's merely the way you like to look at it.

*Director*: I arrived at that metaphor after considerable experience.

*Protégé*: And I'm too young to judge?

*Director*: You're not. But what would you have it be?

*Protégé*: Without metaphor.

*Director*: Okay. The violent are violent. Do you agree?

*Protégé*: I do.

*Director*: And we, we're gentle.

*Protégé*: We are.

*Director*: When the violent meet the gentle, what happens?

*Protégé*: The gentle suffer.

*Director*: The suffering is real?

*Protégé*: Very.

*Director*: Do the violent take pleasure in this?

*Protégé*: They often do.

*Director*: What happens if too much suffering occurs?

*Protégé*: I don't know. What happens?

*Director*: Damage happens.

*Protégé*: Irreversible damage?

*Director*: I've seen it happen.

*Protégé*: How did that make you feel?

*Director*: Sad. And vengeful.


~ VENGEANCE


*Protégé*: But vengeance is dangerous.

*Director*: Why?

*Protégé*: We can get carried away.

*Director*: And do what, too much harm to the violent enemy?

*Protégé*: What kind of harm are we talking about?

*Director*: What kind of harm would you like to talk about?

*Protégé*: Would you do physical harm?

*Director*: I thought we talked about this. All harm is physical, even if it simply comes from words.

*Protégé*: Yes, but you know what I mean.

*Director*: Would I break someone's leg? Yes.

*Protégé*: You see, that's where I can't follow.

*Director*: Why not?

*Protégé*: Honestly? I'm not strong enough to break someone's leg!

*Director*: What about the fact that it's against the law?

*Protégé*: That, too.

*Director*: Then limit yourself to words.

*Protégé*: Why don't you?

*Director*: The violent don't listen to words.

*Protégé*: So you recommend I do something useless?

*Director*: Limit yourself to your clients.

*Protégé*: But then I'm not fighting on the front line with you.

*Director*: Oh, yes you are. You'll help save many from spiritual death. If that's not fighting, I don't know what is.

*Protégé*: I'm a sort of spiritual corpsman, a medic?

*Director*: I think that's a very honorable calling. Don't you?

*Protégé*: I do. But where's my vengeance?

*Director*: It comes in sending your clients back to the fight, stronger.

*Protégé*: But then my vengeance is indirect.

*Director*: You'll have a life outside of work, you know. If you like, fight there, too. There's never a shortage of direct action for those who want it. Just remember to stay in touch with the core.

*Protégé*: I hope you remember.

*Director*: So do I. But why do you bring this up?

*Protégé*: If you delight in killing, you might lose touch.

*Director*: That's true. Can you help me here?

*Protégé*: How?

*Director*: As your client.

*Protégé*: Are you really serious about that?

*Director*: I'm serious.

*Protégé*: Nothing would make me happier! I would do everything in my power to ensure you stay in touch with the core of reason.

*Director*: Then I can rest easy.

*Protégé*: But it will be years before I'm ready!

*Director*: That's okay. You've given me something to look forward to, to hope for. I'll rest in that.


### ~ HOPE


*Protégé*: Is that the only rest we have? In hope?

*Director*: Even in victory, hope is all we have.

*Protégé*: Why?

*Director*: Because we're still vastly outnumbered.

*Protégé*: That can't be all.

*Director*: Even if we weren't outnumbered, we'd still have to fight the enemy within.

*Protégé*: What is that enemy?

*Director*: Fear.

*Protégé*: What would there be for us to fear if we weren't outnumbered?

*Director*: Reason itself.

*Protégé*: Why reason? Because it can turn our world upside down?

*Director*: Among other things, yes. It's a constant courageous effort to stay open to reason.

*Protégé*: So the front line is both without and within?

*Director*: A very good insight. Yes. And the two can blend.

*Protégé*: Then the battle is everywhere. There is no front line.

*Director*: I always said it was just a metaphor.

*Protégé*: But if there is no front line there is no rest!

*Director*: Remember, we rest in hope.

*Protégé*: Where do we find our hope?

*Director*: In ourselves. In others.

*Protégé*: You truly find it in me?

*Director*: I do.

*Protégé*: Well, I find it in you. So we're even. But now I'm scared.

*Director*: Why?

*Protégé*: Because we're talking about actual unremitting warfare.

*Director*: That's life. Can you accept that? Or do you think we're somehow wrong?

*Protégé*: No, everything points to this truth. It just frightens me, is all.

*Director*: You don't have enough hope. I think you'll find it in your clients, when you see what they can overcome.

*Protégé*: I hope so. But aside from me, where do you find hope?

*Director*: In the others I fight for at work, for one. And certain books give me hope. Not many, but some.

*Protégé*: I suppose that has to be good enough.

*Director*: And it is. Too much hope and it would be too easy. That's why we need to strike a balance.

*Protégé*: Between hope and what?

*Director*: Death.

*Protégé*: No, don't say that.

*Director*: Why not?

*Protégé*: Are you talking about our own death?

*Director*: Yes. That's something we can't forget, even—and especially—in the bloom of youth.

*Protégé*: It serves as ballast?

*Director*: Among other things, yes.

*Protégé*: What other things?

*Director*: We don't kill lightly when we remember death.

*Protégé*: Yes, but the 'death' you speak of when you 'kill' isn't actual death.

*Director*: Isn't it?

*Protégé*: You're 'killing' the already 'dead'!

*Director*: Killing the violent, we should say.

*Protégé*: It's the same thing.

*Director*: To 'kill' is to render them inert. Okay? But *Protégé*?

*Protégé*: Yes?

*Director*: The battle is very real.


~ METAPHOR, AGAIN


*Protégé*: Then why speak of a metaphorical battle when it's an actual battle?

*Director*: I didn't want to scare you off.

*Protégé*: Thanks.

*Director*: Oh, don't be upset. Shall we go back and talk about things without the metaphor, see them without that filter?

*Protégé*: I can do that on my own.

*Director*: I hope you will.

*Protégé*: How long have you been fighting this fight?

*Director*: For as long as I can remember.

*Protégé*: And what's the risk to you? That you'll die?

*Director*: Someone might shoot me dead, sure.

*Protégé*: With an actual bullet and gun.

*Director*: Yes. Or a crowd might tear me to pieces. It's happened to philosophers before. Weren't we clear on this?

*Protégé*: I still just find it sort of... shocking.

*Director*: Well, while the violence takes many forms, most often it's in words.

*Protégé*: But if those who speak the words are volatile, and the circumstances are right...

*Director*: ...it goes beyond words.

*Protégé*: So it's better to have a less volatile enemy.

*Director*: Not necessarily. The less volatile are in many ways more dangerous. They're harder to get to. They're often more clever. They work great psychological harm.

*Protégé*: Are you ever tempted to hit them across the head with a board? Surely they deserve it.

*Director*: Yes, but then I'd go to jail.

*Protégé*: They know this and take advantage, don't they?

*Director*: They certainly know their rights.

*Protégé*: Who would you rather fight? The volatile or the less volatile?

*Director*: I fight them all.

*Protégé*: And who will I be fighting?

*Director*: When you're a therapist? Mostly? The enemy within.

*Protégé*: Fear, within my clients. So I'll only be fighting the violent, the ones who harmed them and caused the fear, indirectly.

*Director*: There's a true need for this, my friend. Like I said, I'll make use of your help one day.

*Protégé*: I just can't see me counseling you.

*Director*: Why, because I know so much?

*Protégé*: Yes.

*Director*: You'd be surprised how little I know. I just manage to put it to use.

*Protégé*: Teach me the little you know.

*Director*: I've taught much of it to you today. Learning these things isn't the hard part. Putting them into action is.

*Protégé*: I don't intend to hit anyone with a piece of lumber.

*Director*: Good. Save yourself for the harder fight—the fight for the gentle soul.


~ HELP


*Protégé*: I'll be fighting the harder fight?

*Director*: Of course you will. Don't you know it's easier to fight directly with the enemy?

*Protégé*: Why?

*Director*: Because then you can see exactly how you're doing. The less than direct fight you'll fight gives you precious little insight into what's happening with the violent on the other end. It's very hard to sustain a fight like this.

*Protégé*: I'll have to count on love for my clients to carry me through.

*Director*: Will you love the couple of violent clients you'll keep around?

*Protégé*: Maybe I shouldn't keep them around. After all, I can't help them unless they can help themselves—and most of the violent in this world can't help themselves. Besides, even if I'm able to get them back on their feet, they're only going to go out and do harm to others.

*Director*: You make a good point. But if one of your gentle clients turns violent, what will you do?

*Protégé*: They have harsh words or they bring in a gun?

*Director*: Either.

*Protégé*: In the latter case I disarm them with a board. In the former, I simply persevere.

*Director*: Sounds like you have a plan.

*Protégé*: Well, the real plan is, if someone is threatening me—I'll call you!

*Director*: We can all use some help from time to time. But tell me something, *Protégé*. Is it somehow your fault when you are threatened?

*Protégé*: I know what the violent think about this.

*Director*: What do they think?

*Protégé*: That we live in a way that invites attack.

*Director*: The gentle life of sweet reason invites attack? Why?

*Protégé*: Because the violent think we're weak. And weakness, to them, invites aggression.

*Director*: Are we weak?

*Protégé*: No, I think we're strong, very strong.

*Director*: But the violent mistake us?

*Protégé*: That they do.

*Director*: So they're in for a surprise.

*Protégé*: But why not show our strength in order to prevent the attack?

*Director*: Because showing our strength won't help.

*Protégé*: Why not?

*Director*: Where do we find our strength?

*Protégé*: We find it while in touch with the core.

*Director*: The core speaks softly, yes?

*Protégé*: Yes.

*Director*: Should we shout in response to what we hear from the core?

*Protégé*: No, that wouldn't be fitting.

*Director*: But it might scare the violent away?

*Protégé*: It might.

*Director*: Are you saying it's more important to do the fitting than it is to protect ourselves?

*Protégé*: We need to do the fitting and find other means of protection.

*Director*: What happens if we don't do the fitting?

*Protégé*: While we're busy shouting we can't hear what gentle reason says—and that's the whole point.

*Director*: We must always stay open to reason.

*Protégé*: Yes.

*Director*: Is it ever wrong to be open to reason?

*Protégé*: How could it be?

*Director*: Because safety is our greatest concern.

*Protégé*: No, it can't be.

*Director*: What is our greatest concern?

*Protégé*: Aside from listening to reason? Helping others listen, too.

*Director*: Which others?

*Protégé*: Those who are open to reason.

*Director*: And we're sure this is a greater concern than safety?

*Protégé*: We'd be cowards if it weren't.

*Director*: And so we take our chances.


~ END


*Protégé*: *Director*, how many of the open-to-reason have you seen?

*Director*: Some are open to some things; others are open to others.

*Protégé*: Yes, but how many of the wholly open have you seen?

*Director*: Wholly open? None.

*Protégé*: Not even yourself?

*Director*: When I'm alone, I try to open up all the way. But before I get to that point, I always realize there's more I must learn.

*Protégé*: Learn in order to open up?

*Director*: Yes.

*Protégé*: Can others help you learn?

*Director*: Certainly. But I only try to open all the way when I'm alone.

*Protégé*: Why?

*Director*: Because I'm afraid of my violence, my friend.

*Protégé*: What do you mean?

*Director*: When we open, our violence is there for all to see.

*Protégé*: And you don't want anyone to see your violence.

*Director*: I don't want anyone to suffer from my violence.

*Protégé*: And we all have some violence in us?

*Director*: All of us—all of us, as far as I can tell—have truths we do some violence to. But there is some hope.

*Protégé*: What hope?

*Director*: Fleeting moments.

*Protégé*: What are you talking about?

*Director*: It's possible to share fleeting moments of nearly complete openness.

*Protégé*: Before the violence shows?

*Director*: Just before. And then that's it.

*Protégé*: Then what? We beat a sort of retreat?

*Director*: Yes.

*Protégé*: What a world we live in.

*Director*: But at least we have somewhere to go.

*Protégé*: Where, back to the core?

*Director*: It's the best place to recover.

*Protégé*: Recover and become more strange.

*Director*: But strange to the strange seems normal.

*Protégé*: I wonder how normal we'll seem to the son of the mob.

*Director*: I do, too. So I'd better register for my course. And Protégé?

*Protégé*: Yes?

*Director*: It's not the end of the world if he thinks we're strange.

*Protégé*: No, it's not. But I'll be embarrassed when I next see him in class.

*Director*: You'll have to think your way through the embarrassment.

*Protégé*: I'll try. But I've never done it before.

*Director*: Have you often been embarrassed?

*Protégé*: More than I care to admit.

*Director*: What did you do when you were? Just run away?

*Protégé*: Yes.

*Director*: Well, we won't give in so easily this time. Remember those other two in your class, the interesting ones.

*Protégé*: I will. And you're right. We have to soldier on.

*Director*: Good. And you don't have to worry.

*Protégé*: About what?

*Director*: The price of all that coffee. It's on me.

*Protégé*: How generous of you.

*Director*: You know what they say, don't you?

*Protégé*: No, what?

*Director*: Generous in small things, generous in small things.

*Protégé*: I know you're much more generous than that.

*Director*: Don't go trying to talk me into paying for a lavish dinner.

*Protégé*: You're generous in your patience and time.

*Director*: I really don't see it that way. After all, there's nowhere else I'd rather be.

*Protégé*: Truly?

*Director*: Truly.

*Protégé*: Then I am honored.

*Director*: I am honored.

*Protégé*: We are honored.

*Director*: And we deserve it—because together, alone, we'll win.

Printed in the United States
by Baker & Taylor Publisher Services